The Theory of True Love

YAPING CHEN

Copyright © 2022 Yaping Chen
All rights reserved
First Edition

Fulton Books
Meadville, PA

Published by Fulton Books 2022

ISBN 978-1-63985-550-6 (paperback)
ISBN 978-1-63985-551-3 (digital)

Printed in the United States of America

Contents

Acknowledgments 5
Introduction...7
Chapter 1: True Love and Opposite Attraction 11
Chapter 2: The Theory of True Love: Six Key Principles............14
Chapter 3: How the First Three Principles Influence All
　　　　　　Relationships..21
Chapter 4: Ways of Giving and Receiving.................................28
Chapter 5: Ways of Thinking...41
Chapter 6: The 3D Matrix for the Love Personality 49
Chapter 7: Applying the Theory of True Love to
　　　　　　Existing Romantic Relationships 61
Chapter 8: Improving Parent-Child Relationships with
　　　　　　the Theory of True Love 77
Chapter 9: Finding the Right Romantic Match by
　　　　　　Applying the Theory of True Love 84
Chapter 10: Applying the Theory of True Love to Other
　　　　　　Areas of Life 91
Chapter 11: Identifying Your Personalities 104

Acknowledgments

I want to thank my mother-in-law and father-in-law, Judith Barnard and Michael Fain, who are successful book writers and editors, respectively, for encouraging me to write down my ideas and get my book started. They have always encouraged me when I talked to them about my book or sent them the draft of my book.

Thanks to my husband, Andrew, and my daughter, Janet, who have always supported my idea of writing this book and who provided help with English whenever I needed it; without their love and trust in addition to the unavoidable daily fights, I would not have been able to develop my theory and create this work. Thanks also to my ex-husband, "Sam," and my first true love, Pingping, for without both of them, this theory would have no beginning.

Thanks to my parents, who accidentally made me the "leader" of my family members from the time I was a teenager, planting a strong seed for me to seek the truth and find answers about true love. Even with an incomplete form of my theory, I was able to convince both of my parents to allow me to use our family's story in my book before they passed away. I know they both are very happy for me to have finally finished this book.

Thanks to my dear brother, Zhengyu, for listening to me on WeChat calls, providing insightful ideas for the book, and for his assistance in translating the book into Chinese. Zhengyu always trusted and supported me in writing this book, and from the first time I explained my theory to him, he understood it and enriched it. We both now know that his two key personalities are on the same sides of their continuums as mine!

Thanks to my dear sister, Zhengning, who also gave me her support years ago even though she initially disagreed with my wish to make our family's private life available to anyone who might read my book.

Thanks so much to Betsy Lancefield Lane, my book editor, for her magical work. I am very grateful that my patient-friend Deb connected us with each other. Thanks to David Goderidze, who helped me edit the first draft, and to Jake Loewenheim and my daughter, Janet (again), for their insightful feedback on that initial draft, which was not easy to read.

Thanks to all the angels—I could not name everyone here—that God sent me to strengthen my belief at all the right times. Without you, my initial theory would have been abandoned long ago and never developed into the theory presented on these pages.

Thanks to each person I encountered in depth sometime in my life. You may love me, hate me, or have mixed feelings about me because of my love and assistance to you, my mistakes, or my actions that were borne of who I was at that time. In either a positive or negative way, you helped shape who I am today and therefore helped develop this theory. If by any chance you were to ask for my assistance in the future, I promise to try my best to support you better than I could in the past—by applying this theory!

Thanks to all my patients who trusted me and allowed me to work with them by applying my theory of true love to improve their relationships. This helped reduce their stress around romantic or familial relationships. Along with their acupuncture treatments, my theory helped my patients achieve significant improvements in both their physical and mental well-being. Many of my patients told me, "You have magical hands!" In fact, my "magical hands" often need my secret weapon—the help of the application of my theory to reduce their emotional stress level. Some of my patients never noticed this secret weapon while others realized they were simultaneously benefitting from acupuncture as well as being able to talk with me during those treatments, which also helped them feel better. Some of them even brought their boyfriends or girlfriends to appointments and asked for my honest opinions, and some would come to me for advice when their relationships weren't going well. The encouragement of my most recent patients, who benefitted from the latest version of my theory of true love, is especially meaningful to me.

Introduction

This book is to help you improve your relationships of any kind: romantic relationships, parent-child relationships, working relationships, friendships, and so on. If you're hoping to enter a romantic relationship, the book will help you discover the key characteristics of your most suitable partner, choose the most suitable person, and avoid impossible or inefficient long-term romantic relationships. In relationships you cannot choose—such as family—the book will help you make improvements to reduce feelings of stress, strain, or other difficulties. And if you have been married for years but are not very happy with each other, applying my theory of true love might just change your life.

My theory of true love began about thirty years ago when I went through a very difficult breakup process. That's a long story and deserves a book all its own. In a nutshell, that "life and death" breakup experience helped me discover a few critical human natures, which I call my theory of true love. The theory has led me to a much deeper understanding of all kinds of relationships, and I have realized this theory is very important for managing parent-child relationships in which two opposite personalities exist—as we'll discover later in this book. The theory might also be helpful for improving management systems, including political systems. It has something to offer to any situation in which two or more people are working together.

The theory begins by helping you recognize your own strengths and weaknesses to make better choices in life. We all have unique talents based on our natural personalities. True love with full acceptance—from ourselves as well as from others—is the foundation of self-confidence. We all need to love and be loved.

Since finishing the first draft of this book in September 2020, my business relationships have become more efficient by applying my theory freely. As a holistic acupuncturist practicing in the San Francisco Bay Area, the theory helps me be more efficient in helping my patients with their relationship issues. As you'll see, I think many disagreements between people are caused by those people's opposing personalities. I hope reading this book will help more people understand and apply this theory as it will help keep small disagreements from becoming larger conflicts between individuals, groups, or even countries. I have applied my theory successfully in helping resolve some difficult conflicts, including some that went through the courts and legal system.

Focusing on developing each person's personality-related strengths and improving on their personality-related weaknesses—not the other way around—is the most effective and desirable way for individuals to develop and grow. Understanding the two opposites of the personalities described in this book is critical for children's education and development in schools and at home, and so is identifying and accepting the related strengths and weaknesses of each.

The theory of true love also challenges some important concepts of traditional Confucianism, especially the beliefs that teaching and education are the keys to shaping people's behaviors and that humans are born unselfish beings (*ren zi chu, xin ben san*). Respecting one's natural personalities is as important as teaching and education.

This book also raises some challenging questions, such as the following:

- Is Chinese medicine less important than Western medicine due to the lack of scientific research on traditional Chinese medicine?
- Should we require students to study hard-to-quantify subjects such as relationships and parenting? These courses, if successful, could affect our society tremendously from generation to generation.
- Is the diagnosis of ADD or ADHD possibly a mistake?

- Should parenting be more like a professional service, allowing children with insurmountable difficulties with their birth parents (resulting from their two opposite personalities) to grow up in a way more naturally aligned with the child's personality?
- Is it possible that you might be happier living in China instead of the United States? Is the current political system in the United States more advanced than China's political system? You will find my thoughts on these questions in chapter 10.

There are countless other questions raised and possible applications, but I will focus mainly on the applications of my theory of true love in two key areas: romantic relationships and parent-child relationships.

In the following pages, we'll explore the law of opposite attraction and the six key principles that form the foundation of my theory. These include three basic principles and three sets of personality types—two sets of opposite personalities for relationships of any kind and a third specifically for romantic relationships. We'll also discuss different ways of giving and receiving love (which I believe to be genetically determined); divergent ways of thinking for learning, communicating, and understanding; and the complex, personality-based needs of emotional and physical love (both sexual and nonsexual) for romantic relationships. Then, you can complete a questionnaire designed to help you identify your own three personality styles and how to apply the theory of true love in your own life.

And if you'd like, you will have the opportunity to help me develop the theory of true love further. Because my own experiences and my access to other people's personal experiences are naturally limited, the methods I have developed will likely be improved over time as more people apply the theory in their own lives to help themselves or others. I welcome this feedback as it will help me gather more different combinations of the three personalities, allowing others to conduct additional studies on the topic. If you have suggestions or ideas to share with me, please send me an email (yaping@thetheoryoftruelove.com). I will be grateful for your feedback. If you share my passion and would like to work together with me to enhance and spread this theory and its applications, please visit thetheoryoftruelove.com. Also, if you need my help for your current romantic relationship issues or if you need my help to identify your personality types, please go to the website and follow the instructions.

I am enthusiastic about problem-solving for relationships and developing my theory further to better understand the three key personalities and their roles in people's talents, their limitations, children's development, and their effects on relationships; and I'd like to continue to study how the three different personalities influence the likelihood of success in romantic relationships.

Chapter 1

True Love and Opposite Attraction

Do you often make self-sacrifices for your loved ones or other people? Do you have difficulty saying no to friends? Do you believe in true love for romantic relationships? Are you a selfish person or an unselfish one? This last one is a classic question, and you probably already have an answer in mind. After you read this book, you may have a different answer.

Almost every action has both selfish and unselfish aspects, just as even the best things in life often come with a negative aspect or consequence. Everyone who survives within a community has both selfish and unselfish aspects, and in reality, nobody should be completely selfish or unselfish!

My father once told me, "All romantic love is selfish. Only the love of parents for their children is selfless." I did not agree with my father, but I could not provide my argument at that time. With the theory in this book, now I could tell my father that I believe both romantic and parental love have selfish and unselfish aspects.

I believe that, by nature, we all have both selfish and unselfish aspects to our personalities, as I'll explain in chapter 2. People naturally need to love and to be loved. But each one of us may give love and want to be loved differently based on our different personalities, as we'll see later on. In fact, the two people in a romantic relationship may love each other in ways completely opposite from each other. These differences can discourage one or both partners' unselfish aspects and encourage their selfish aspects, causing many people to question whether true love exists at all. But each one of us is unique and needs to be accepted fully by ourselves and by the people we love. This is the foundation for our self-confidence. It is not always easy, and at times it can feel unbelievably challenging. This book will provide you a road map and the tools you need to master this process.

Most people doubt the possibility of true, lasting love or at least don't believe in it outright. Some say that the experience of being in love can only last a couple of years at most, and after that, the honeymoon is over. Some think this type of love is romanticized and only exists in books and movies, not in real life.

I used to be among these doubters. However, this all changed after a few dramatic events in my late twenties, and thus, my belief in true love sprouted and grew strong. I became aware that true love actually *does* exist, and it's much more available than most people realize. People's ability to stay in love *can* last more than several months or years, and in fact, it can become even deeper and more powerful with time. This kind of love will surely last forever because the relationship naturally forms a positive feedback system, which will be explained more later in this book. Yet not everyone wants this kind of love (for example, highly independent people can feel trapped, smothered, or stressed by it), and even people who *do* want this kind of romantic relationship may not be aware that it has its own imperfect aspect. Namely, this type of romantic relationship between two people can cause both to lose their own identities as they become united into a "merged" version of two individuals. Some people refer to their spouse as their other half, but if half of you were literally missing, obviously, it would be very difficult to continue being happy or living a normal life. In chapter 2, we'll look at ways the life-or-death feeling of some romantic love can be problematic if both partners are of the "blending"-type personality and, therefore, struggle to protect their own love needs in the relationship.

It was in my late twenties when I realized my desire to prove this concept to myself. With the guidance of my own theory about the secret of true love, I thought I would be able to start and build new relationships that were fulfilling and harmonized with fewer struggles and less pain. But I was wrong again! I still had some work to do.

THE THEORY OF TRUE LOVE

In the past twenty years of my life, in my second marriage, I have still experienced some serious struggles occasionally, and in fact, I almost lost my own belief in true love. Fortunately, with the help of my theory, I was able to survive the most difficult periods, learn from them, and continue to develop my theory.

While working on my second marriage, I also struggled with my relationship with my daughter, Janet, who I brought up by myself from the time she was three years old. She turned out to have inherited her key personalities from her birth father, and these were opposite of my own. The struggles of my relationship with Janet nearly left me defeated, but they also helped me develop and finalize my theory of true love.

So one challenge is the attraction of opposites, which we'll explore throughout the book. Another relationship challenge stems from the unquantifiable nature of human beings, which also makes a romantic relationship difficult. Love is unquantifiable. Many people do not know the exact type of love they need from a romantic relationship when they are young. At some point, they may have felt they were "in love" with someone, but later the feeling was gone. They thought the explanation was that they had changed, but it is most often the unquantifiable nature of love that caused the confusion rather than a change of themselves and their romantic needs.

Each person gives love and receives love differently. This coupled with the unquantifiable nature of love makes it hard for us to clearly identify our needs (or our partner's) either in quality or quantity. What we want from our romantic partner may require a complicated learning process. Some of us may need one or more failed love experiences to know our own needs. Only a very small percentage of us are lucky enough to fall in love with the right person in our first romantic relationship.

In the following chapters, I share my key findings about true love to help you learn more about yourself and your love needs based on your personalities. With the guidance of this theory, you will learn and appreciate more from all your romantic experiences, *especially* the unsuccessful or difficult ones. You will enjoy and explore romantic relationships more freely and eventually find your true love, if that is your desire.

Chapter 2

The Theory of True Love: Six Key Principles

My theory of true love consists of six principles. The first three are general principles, the next two define two sets of opposite personalities that apply to relationships of any kind, and the sixth defines a love personality that applies to romantic relationships.

Principle 1: selfish and unselfish aspects

All humans are born with both selfish and unselfish aspects of their natures. The selfish aspect is aimed at the individual's survival, and the unselfish aspect involves working with others. A successful relationship requires a healthy balance of both. Finding this balance of selfishness and selflessness between two people in a long-term romantic relationship is key to the happiness of both partners.

Similarly, in the workplace, a successful management system requires two sets of rules: one set to promote selflessness and the other to limit selfishness, enabling each party to form a balanced feedback system. The two sets of rules are equally important.

In the political arena, the political system in the United States is strong in limiting people's selfishness but weaker in promoting people's selflessness. The Chinese political system is the opposite; it is stronger in encouraging people's selflessness but weaker in limiting people's selfishness. Therefore, both systems have their own strengths and weaknesses.

I was born in China and grew up there until I moved to the United States in my late twenties. I discovered my initial theory of true love while I was in China, but the years in America made it possible for me to complete it. Living in and being influenced by two such opposite political systems also allowed me to think about how balancing selfish and unselfish tendencies might be applied to our legal and political systems; this is discussed in chapter 10.

Principle 2: opposite attraction

The law of opposite attraction applies to many human relationships, especially upon initial contact. Most romantic relationships begin with two people who have opposite personalities to some degree. The greater the difference between their personalities the stronger the initial attraction will generally be. Therefore, most romantic relationships naturally form a negative feedback system between the two parties. Without understanding the key personality differences, many relationships start with love but end in frustration or even hatred toward each other.

Principle 3: quantifiable and unquantifiable natures

Both the quantifiable and the unquantifiable aspects of humans are equally important. Love is unquantifiable; it cannot truly be measured. This naturally means that romantic relationships, being based on love, can also be difficult to measure, and it will be difficult to know when we've achieved the state of balance between selflessness and selfishness (as required by the first principle). It is important to find peace with the unquantifiable nature of love.

As we just noted, many relationships built on the law of opposite attraction form negative feedback systems. These situations are also difficult to measure and quantify and difficult for most people to define or describe in useful ways to their romantic partners. Thus, many romantic relationships that become negative tend to stay that way, and the relationships ultimately fail due to both a lack of balance *and* an inability to define, discuss, and remedy the situation. The failure is not due to a lack of true love from both sides but rather the opposite personalities preventing one or both sides to *feel* loved.

Hard science (such as biology and chemistry) requires experiments and data. Scientific studies tend to focus on the quantifiable aspects of human nature, resulting in a bias in favor of emphasizing (and researching) only the quantifiable aspects of life. Although unquantifiable aspects of human behavior are inherently harder to define, they are no less important.

The subject of love and developing healthy relationships should be an important subject taught to children as early as elementary school, yet there is no curriculum on this subject. The reasons likely range from a cultural tendency to avoid controversially personal or private topics (like relationships) in public schools to a lack of time in a school calendar already filled with curricular requirements to a lack of science-based course content developed for this audience. The truth is, humans are born with both quantifiable and unquantifiable traits, and we need to recognize and respect both. The earlier we learn this the healthier our relationships can be. We've made a start with anti-bullying education, which is a good place to begin.

In medicine, again we find very different models in the United States and China. Whereas Western medicine focuses mainly on the quantifiable aspects of health, traditional Chinese medicine focuses more on the unquantifiable aspects. Both systems have strengths and weaknesses, and the combination of both approaches provides a more complete medical health system for all. Depending on the nature of the problem, one modality may be more helpful than the other, and some conditions may require both modalities to bring the patient relief. It is promising to see that some health insurance plans are beginning to cover certain traditional Chinese medicine treatments—a trend I hope will continue to grow over time as both systems are equally important for human health.

THE THEORY OF TRUE LOVE

Principle 4: giving and receiving

Humans are born with two opposite ways of giving and receiving, and these define the most important pair of opposite personalities. Each person falls somewhere along a continuum between two opposite ways of giving and receiving love. It is my belief that this position along the continuum is genetic and thus stronger than simply a (good or bad) habit. However, because this is poorly understood, most people blame their own, their children's, or their romantic partner's "bad habits" for relationship problems. This misses the point and only creates more relationship problems.

The two opposite styles of giving and receiving sometimes make it nearly impossible for people in love to form a balanced system, as required by the first principle. I use the words *blending* and *independent* to describe the two opposite ways of giving and receiving love. Each of these personality types incorporates selfish and unselfish aspects in their unique ways, and each has its own strengths and weaknesses. This will be discussed further in chapter 4.

Depending on how close the romantic partners' personalities are, a positive, negative, or balanced feedback system could form naturally between them. The fourth principle explains why many romantic relationships fail and why some become more negative despite great (yet ineffective) effort from both sides.

One final note about principle 4 is this: two people with the blending-type personality could be expected to form a positive feedback system naturally, but they have little opportunity to become a couple in the first place because either the law of opposite attraction leads them away from each other or other personality traits are not in favor of them being romantically involved as a couple. I will explain this interesting phenomenon more in chapter 9.

Principle 5: linear and nonlinear thinking

Humans are born with two opposite ways of thinking: linear and nonlinear thinking. This is the second most important pair of opposite personalities for relationships of any kind. The two opposite ways of thinking (linear and nonlinear) lead each person to different ways of learning or gaining knowledge and to different ways of understanding others through communication.

Our society has traditionally emphasized linear thinking and treats it as the sole way of thinking for each and every person. The nonlinear way of thinking is the minority and is largely ignored. We try to teach everyone the linear way of thinking. Our education system favors linear thinkers. We designed our courses, especially those in math and science, to be taught mainly with the linear way of thinking in mind even though many great scientific discoveries were the result of flashes of insight, dreams, and other types of nonlinear thinking.

Reading is another common activity that highlights how differences in the thinking personality can make a significant difference in one's learning. Your thinking personality can heavily influence which authors you find interesting and even which books you find easier to read and learn from. For example, my daughter, Janet, and I are on opposite sides of the thinking personality, and we tend to like very different books. When Janet eagerly recommends books to me, I always try to read them. Unfortunately, I consistently find her book recommendations put me to sleep, or it takes me a long time to finish them. Similarly, when I recommend a book to Janet, she often ends up telling me that she just couldn't get through it or that it was too boring for her. No matter how much we want to read and enjoy each other's book recommendations, we often give up long before we finish.

The two opposite ways of thinking also define different ways of understanding and communicating. This makes it difficult (and at times nearly impossible) for essential communication to occur in relationships of any kind. Effective communication is critical in any relationship both for understanding others and explaining how we think and feel. If the people in a relationship have two opposite ways of thinking, they will have difficulty understanding each other in daily communications no matter how hard they try. This places a great strain on relationships and sometimes causes them to fail.

I believe we are wrong to treat linear thinking as the primary way of thinking for all people and that we have made mistakes in treating extreme cases of natural, nonlinear thinking as a psychological problem, labeling it attention deficit disorder (ADD) or attention deficit hyperactivity disorder (ADHD). There have always been historical geniuses with ADD or ADHD who have shown their talent in nontraditional ways.

Students who are not genetically predisposed to linear thinking may have trouble learning in school. They are often diagnosed with ADHD when they are young. Students with less extreme tendencies toward nonlinear thinking might not be diagnosed with ADD/ADHD but still struggle to learn academic content. At some point, these students might start to doubt themselves or wonder whether they have ADD/ADHD. Some young people start self-medicating with any number of questionable "cures" to help them focus on studying for exams in order to perform "normally." I strongly suggest further research be done based on this theory of the nonlinear personality type.

Principle 6: emotional love and physical love (and the 3D matrix of a love personality)

The third important aspect of a love personality is for romantic relationships—the complex 3D matrix of emotional and physical love. Physical love includes both sexual and nonsexual love.

In addition to the third and fourth principles, this personality difference makes it more difficult for many of us to define our needs in romantic relationships clearly. As long-term romantic partners, we need to consider these complex needs together with the opposite ways of giving and receiving and opposite ways of thinking. We now have many possible combinations of personalities in romantic relationships, and it can be very difficult for two people to determine if they are the right match for each other. This explains why, on some popular dating shows on television, two people fall truly in love and then often feel confused when they realize they made the wrong choice, breaking up soon afterward even though some of them were provided with plenty of potential partners and quality time to find the best match. If these and other people (especially those who think in linear ways) seeking love were aware of the theory I present in this book, I think they could learn to identify red flags quickly and achieve better relationship results.

The third principle—the unquantifiable nature of all three personalities—makes it very difficult for an individual to identify optimal (or even workable) long-term romantic partners. Some people may need plenty of experiences and time to learn about their own needs in romantic love elsewhere. This process will be more difficult still for those who are already in a relationship and have a way of thinking that's opposite to that of their partner.

Each of the three personalities is so critical to success, and each will be explained in greater detail in a chapter of its own where you'll also learn to recognize the red, yellow, and green lights to help you identify the most—and least—workable combinations.

CHAPTER 3

How the First Three Principles Influence All Relationships

Now that we've covered the six principles in brief, let's take a closer look at the first principle. Then we'll discuss the importance of the first three principles working together in relationships of any kind.

Let me start with some stories from the very beginning of the theory of true love.

One year, around 1980, when I was attending university in China, the country had an extended, nationwide debate on the topic "Are humans genetically selfish or unselfish?" The debate went on for many months in newspapers, college student meetings, gatherings of different sizes, and so on. Both sides made strong arguments supported by many examples of people who were either selfish or unselfish. By the end of the debate, there was no conclusion. I was not convinced either way, and since I had no clear answer at that time, I carried the question in my mind.

In 1987, at my wedding to my first husband (we'll call him Sam), one of my friends asked, "Since you two have been living in two different cities for the past four years, did you miss each other while you were apart?" My answer was, "Yes, of course." My brand-new husband answered, "No, I did not."

After the wedding, several of my friends came to me and asked me if Sam even cared about me, adding, "He sounds selfish. How could you marry him?" I defended him: "It is how he deals with the situations, by not thinking of me to focus on other important stuff. He is not a bad person. At least he does not lie in such a special occasion with so many of my friends!"

In 1988, Sam was preparing to come to the United States to study for his PhD in physics. One day, he and I went to visit my very dear friend Beiyan. She told us that there was a new government policy about going out to other countries, especially the United States, for higher education, which might affect Sam's plan. She offered to make a copy of the policy document for him, but Sam immediately refused with a simple no and no other explanation. Beiyan was shocked and felt uncomfortable. She looked at me. I felt embarrassed. Soon afterward, we said goodbye to my friend. As soon as we left my friend's house, I asked Sam, "Why did you refuse my friend's kind offer of making a copy of the document for you?" He replied, "I thought you could easily to do it. Why should I waste her time for such a small thing?" I was relieved and called my friend to explain things when I got back home. She felt better too and started seeing him differently and less antagonistically.

One day in 1991, while Sam was in his graduate program in the United States, he mentioned that his professor seemed unhappy with Sam driving his own car to work at a research center some distance away. There was a car for the two graduate students to share. The other student only used the shared car, but Sam sometimes used his own vehicle. His professor asked him to use the shared car several times, but since the other student used the shared car frequently, it was difficult to coordinate times they could share it. Sam explained to me that using his personal vehicle was a way to avoid conflicts with the other student. When I asked him why he did not explain this to his professor, Sam said, "The professor is busy enough. Why should I bother him with such a small thing and have him worry about it?"

Later, I managed to sit beside the professor during a group gathering, and I struck up a conversation in which I briefly explained the reason behind the "car using" issue. The professor thanked me sincerely because he had grown frustrated with Sam's "bad" behavior. After my explanation, the professor was happy, and the problem resolved. Understanding Sam's reasoning also increased the respect the professor had for him.

My marriage to Sam was difficult at times. I often felt hurt by and disappointed in him. I tried to talk to him about it, sometimes at length. He always listened quietly without responding. I assumed he agreed with me at least to some extent since I would provide some of my opinions if the tables were turned and I did not agree with him. Yet even after those long talks, I saw no change in Sam's behavior. Sometimes, out of frustration, I would say to him, "How could you be so selfish?" Again, he was silent, which I interpreted as agreement that he was behaving selfishly.

One day, Sam turned my accusation of selfishness back on me, saying that I was sometimes selfish too. I was surprised! At that moment, I realized my actions had their own selfish aspects when seen from another person's point of view. Principle 1 sprouted when I realized that my behaviors had a selfish aspect—just as Sam's "selfish" behaviors also had a selfless aspect.

It gradually became clear to me that it was a big mistake for us to think that people are either selfish or unselfish by nature. I finally had my answer to the question I had carried for more than a decade.

Years later, when arguing with my daughter, out of frustration, I would sometimes ask, "Can you just appreciate what I did for you?" or, "Can you please at least appreciate the time I am sacrificing for you?" She would answer, "I did not expect your appreciation for anything I did for you!" or, "I do not want your sacrifice. Please only spend time with me when you want to!" I can guarantee you that we will repeat this exchange in the future. It is how our minds work differently because of our personality. This kind of conflict stemming from personality differences can never be entirely eliminated.

One day, I was at the beach, writing some ideas for this book, when my daughter, Janet, joined me and started asking me for some relationship advice. I was eager to get back to my writing, but I did not tell her. I tend to set aside my own projects and start helping people, especially my daughter, whenever I feel I am needed. However, in those situations, I am generally tense and impatient, and it can result in me raising my voice unintentionally. On that day at the beach, I must have raised my voice again at Janet when I was giving her my opinion. This seemed to upset her. Similar situations had happened between us already time and time again. We had both previously agreed to try to avoid these situations, but we always failed.

This time, I again reminded her that my raised voice was just my natural way of trying to explain my ideas. I was not angry with her, and my opinion might not have even been the best one for her. I only wanted her to understand my ideas to see if they would be helpful for her. However, when Janet hears this voice of mine, she thinks that I am really angry and yelling at her. For context, Janet likes to speak more softly and slowly, and she is more deliberate with her words. So what I think is my "normal" raised voice might come off as angry to her ears. She has repeatedly told me that when I raise my voice, it hurts her ears and is not the best way to communicate with her. Unfortunately, when I try to explain things to her, my passion overcomes me, and sometimes it just comes off too strong toward my beloved daughter. I truly only want the best for her.

On that day, keeping in mind the natural differences between the two of us, I realized that I needed to lower my voice, so I tried my best to calm down and speak softly. I said, "I am sorry for my voice, but can you just ignore my raised voice and focus on understanding what I am trying to explain to you?"

Janet replied, "You are still expecting me to understand you first. It's a double standard!"

At that moment, I stopped talking and helplessly walked away from her. I was very frustrated with myself for making the same mistake again. Since I first drafted this book, I had established a strict rule for myself, promising myself not to give Janet relationship advice face-to-face. But I did it again! I told myself, "Without expecting Janet to understand what I'm explaining to her, what is the point of spending my precious time trying to do so? It would be a complete waste of both of our time. I have to follow my own rule strictly and avoid face-to-face conversations in which I try to explain my ideas to Janet." But at the same time, I had to admit something uncomfortable; namely, Janet had just pointed out that my expectation for *her*

THE THEORY OF TRUE LOVE

to understand *me* does in fact have a selfish aspect. I have no right to expect this from her.

Like many times before, this argument with Janet turned into one of the best examples for me to use when explaining my theory. This one in particular was a good example of the selfish and unselfish aspects of personalities coexisting together. Doing things for others with no expectation of anything in return is part of Janet's personality, and it is unselfish. Expecting an understanding of my ideas and an appreciation for the time it takes me to explain it is part of my personality and has a selfish aspect to it. Again, our opposite personalities both have selfish and unselfish aspects.

Everyone has both selfish and unselfish aspects to their natures. Because the two opposite ways of giving and receiving love both have selfish and unselfish aspects, they both have their own strengths and weaknesses. No one should be forced to switch to the opposite end of the continuum; they must coexist. In other words, no one can be completely selfish or completely unselfish. The selfish side of the continuum is for self-protection and survival, and the unselfish side is for living with others. Selfishness and unselfishness are seen differently from different perspectives.

A relationship between two people is the smallest multiperson relationship, of course, whether the relationship is romantic, managerial, or between a parent and child. Based on the selfish and unselfish aspects and for the relationship to last, it should not become a negative feedback system. Any such relationship requires two sets of rules: those to promote each person's unselfish side and those to limit each person's selfish side. Balanced relationships should be fair to all people involved, asking all parties to adapt for the greater good: the healthy functioning of the relationship or system.

Receiving true love with full acceptance of one's natural personality is the key to self-confidence for many people. The need to receive love from others is equivalent to the need for acceptance by others. The need to give love to others is equivalent to the need to survive by cooperating with others to meet life's challenges. Therefore, most people genetically need to love and to be loved at the same time unless one lives in isolation forever.

Unfortunately, without understanding the differences between opposite personalities, many people grow up in families with parents who struggle with themselves as well as with their children. Examples of true love with full acceptance are rare in life, and sadly, poor parenting practices often get passed along, largely unchanged, from generation to generation. Many parents try to change their children's natural personalities unsuccessfully, which in fact does more harm than good.

Because of principle 2 (the attraction of opposites), many romantic relationships start with a negative feedback system that is unable to promote selflessness or limit selfishness in one or both partners. When we then add principle 3 (the unquantifiable nature of love), we can understand why most relationship issues are difficult to define, communicate, and resolve.

With the three sets of opposite personalities described in principles 4, 5, and 6, only some negative feedback systems can be changed into balanced systems with proper effort. Some other negative feedback systems are too problematic to bring into balance no matter how hard both sides try.

A completely balanced system for a love relationship should last forever. A positive feedback system will bring each partner's unselfish side forward since both partners receive what they need and are motivated to give more back to the other. A negative feedback system will bring out one partner's selfish side more as a self-protection mechanism for survival. Sometimes a negative feedback system brings out the selfish side in both partners. Since both partners are deprived of what they need from the relationship, their selfish sides continually grow stronger, and the negative feedback system becomes even more negative with time.

Principles 1 through 3, taken together, address human nature as the foundation of relationships of any kind. They provide the foundation for applying principles 4 through 6 in addressing relationship issues.

The role of mediators or therapists is to help the people in the relationship (individually or jointly) understand the reasons for conflict and guide them toward positive directions for solutions. This is often very helpful. However, sometimes the questions or words from mediators or therapists can prompt more negativity or greater doubts between the two parties, depending on the specific issues the couple is having with communication and the counselor's own communication style. From my observation, many conflicts in relationships start with disagreement stemming from personality differences. These conflicts are unavoidable, and they are difficult to resolve since it is inherently hard for people on opposite ends of the personality continuums to understand each other. Once the underlying personality differences are clearly understood, it is easier for both partners to accept the differences and move on. I believe my theory could become a useful new tool for mediators and therapists working with people in challenging relationships.

Understanding the theory and the personality differences may be a key to avoiding, minimizing, or resolving many conflicts caused by opposite personalities. I hope this book will help more people begin to understand this theory and develop true love toward themselves and others by accepting personality differences. This would increase the chances for a peaceful world for all of us, with less likelihood that relatively small disagreements will become bigger conflicts or even destructive wars.

Chapter 4

Ways of Giving and Receiving

Every human gives and receives love differently. Each of us is born somewhere along a continuum between two opposite ways of giving and receiving love. The two opposite ends of this continuum—the blending end and the "independent" end—form a strong negative feedback system. The opposite attraction between two people at the opposite ends of this spectrum may initially be so strong that it draws them together into an impossible long-term romantic relationship.

Most people fall somewhere between the two ends of the giving-receiving spectrum, which means some romantic relationships will work with minimal effort and some with more significant effort while some will be too difficult to sustain no matter how much effort each person invests in it.

Each person's innate way of giving love should decide the way they receive love. Giving and receiving should be equal for a person to be balanced and survive. But we grow up in various cultural or religious contexts, most of which teach us to give more and receive less. Some people learn this and become more selfless as a result. Some cannot learn it and stay the way they were born, which is where they feel balanced. Still, others learn the opposite, giving less and receiving more, and become more selfish; narcissists are the extreme example of this.

Individuals at one end of the spectrum might describe themselves by saying, "I give whenever others need from me. Most often, this requires self-sacrifice or inconveniencing myself." In contrast, individuals at the opposite end of the spectrum would be more likely to say, "I give only when I want to and never make self-sacrifices or inconvenience myself." Naturally, most people's way of giving falls somewhere between these two extremes. Only rarely is someone's way of giving at or very close to either of these opposite ends.

Ideally, people's ways of receiving would exactly match their ways of giving, thus creating balance. It is obvious that if an individual gives to others whenever she or he is needed, always making self-sacrifices for others, then this person would be likely to assume others will do the same. On the other hand, if one gives only whenever one feels like it, never making self-sacrifices for others, this person will naturally assume others will be the same.

To describe all the possibilities of giving and receiving, we could imagine a graph of two straight lines. On this graph, imagine the x-axis plots giving while the y-axis plots receiving. As we begin plotting hypothetical combinations—high giving and low receiving, low giving and high receiving, moderate giving and high receiving, and so on—we quickly see there are an infinite number of possibilities on our graph and that giving and receiving are actually quite hard to quantify.

What I have found from applying this theory is that the vast majority of individuals have styles of giving and receiving that are nearly the same. Because of this, and to make the theory easy to apply, I assume that an individual's way of giving and way of receiving are exactly the same. Here's why this works: Even when a person's way of giving and way of receiving is not exactly the same, they are quite close to each other. This makes sense because if there is no balance between a person's way of giving and way of receiving, the individual is either too easily taken advantage of or too selfish to be in an ongoing romantic relationship.

Interestingly, I have found that those people whose way of giving is in the middle often have their way of receiving just a bit off to either side but not too far away. People who fall toward the blending side of giving are likely to have their way of receiving also on the blending side. The same holds true for people on the independent side; their way of giving and of receiving are likely both on that same side.

Let's look at two examples.

First, imagine a person who always gives love to others with no expectation of receiving love from others in return. This person would not be able to learn how to ask for or receive love in a relationship and only knows how to give it. Is there any chance this person will stay the same and survive forever? In a relationship, this person won't last long, and this is also teaching the other partner to become completely selfish, only taking love without giving any back.

Next, consider the opposite: a person who never makes self-sacrifices for others yet expects others to sacrifice for him or her. Even if this person succeeds, this relationship can only last for a short time. Before long, people will recognize this person's selfishness and stop helping. This person won't survive in a long-term relationship either.

To make it even easier to apply this concept when discussing relationships, I imagine the giving continuum as a straight line with five points from left to right—a basic number line—with two points on either side and one point in the middle. Each point on this line is referred to as a level: from left to right, the points represent level 1 to level 5, or simply G1 through G5 (*G* because this is the "giving" continuum). People at each of these levels will identify with the statement given for that level below:

- G1: I mostly give help to others only when I want to and am unlikely to inconvenience myself to do so.
- G2: I often give help to others when I want to, and sometimes I might inconvenience myself to do so.
- G3, the middle level: About half the time, I try to give help whenever others need it, but half the time, I only give help if it is convenient for me to do so.
- G4: I often give help whenever others need it, and I often make self-sacrifices to do so; sometimes, though, I only give help when I want to.
- G5: I almost always give help whenever others need it, willingly making self-sacrifices almost all the time.

THE THEORY OF TRUE LOVE

We can now clearly see the two opposite ends (G1 and G5), the middle or balanced level (G3), and the two intermediate sides (G2 and G4, independent and blending, respectively). The independent side, on the left, includes G1 and G2. The blending side, on the right, includes G4 and G5. Which side a person belongs to is more important than their exact position on the number line until you get to the two poles (G1 and G5).

I call G1 and G2 the independent personality and G4 and G5 the blending personality. I also call the two ends (G1 and G5) the independent end and the blending end, respectively.

Both blending and independent personalities have their own strengths and weaknesses. I believe these personalities are genetic and difficult to change—far more difficult than simply asking someone to change a bad habit. Generally, both nature and nurture influence these personalities. Forcing someone to change his or her personality side is not only unhelpful but can also be destructive.

Calling people with independent personality selfish is a mistake, and it needs to be corrected. If we only focus on the giving part of the equation, it seems that people with the G5 personality are unselfish and the people with the G1 personality selfish. But this is not true.

We can see this when we consider the levels (G1 through G5) as a combination of giving and receiving. In this light, both G1 and G5 people have their own selfish and unselfish aspects. The G5 personality gives with sacrifices (unselfish) but, at the same time, expects the other side to make sacrifices either for them, their family, or their country (selfish). The sacrifices made by G5 personalities are known as sacrifices with expectations. For their part, the G1 people make no sacrifices for others (selfish), but they also do not expect anyone to make sacrifices for them (unselfish). This is known as giving without condition or expectation.

We now see that both G1 and G5 personalities embody selfish and unselfish aspects. This is why I use the words *independent* and *blending* rather than *selfish* and *unselfish* for the two opposite ways of giving and receiving. This finding lies at the very foundation of my theory of true love.

In romantic relationships, blending personalities are likely to be:

- more willing and better able to make self-sacrifices or self-adjustments based on their partner's needs,
- sensitive to their partner's needs,
- better at group activities,
- more considerate of how other people think,
- more willing and better able to bend the rules,
- weaker at protecting themselves,
- slower to recognize their own needs since they are more open to adapting to others' needs first,
- weaker in defending what is best for themselves,
- less confident,
- more troubled by saying no,
- have expectations of others, and
- easily disappointed.

On the other hand, independent personalities in romantic relationships are likely to be

- more familiar with what they want;
- strong in self-protection;
- self-confident;
- free of expectations that any help, service, or gifts they give to others will be reciprocated;
- good at establishing and maintaining boundaries;
- in need of more time alone;
- good at following rules;
- strict in enforcing laws;
- insensitive to other's needs;
- unable to recognize conflicts or problems;
- slow to act on an issue until action becomes unavoidable and then explode;
- rude or hurtful to others who disturb them; and
- less willing or able to make self-sacrifices.

If the two people in a romantic relationship both have a blending personality, their relationship should form a naturally positive feedback system. Both partners are sensitive to each other's needs and will make self-sacrifices for the other. This kind of love will easily last a long time. This love relationship may eventually merge the two people into one, making it overwhelmingly difficult for either person to live a normal life without the other partner.

Similarly, if two people in a romantic relationship share independent personality, their relationship should be balanced and reasonably free of conflict; both sides have their own space. This type of relationship should also last a long time. Both parties will keep their own identities, never blending together into one even after many years together.

However…

Life doesn't always work out so smoothly. Based on the second principle, the law of opposite attraction, it is most likely that two people in a romantic relationship have opposite personalities when it comes to giving and receiving love, and because of this, a negative feedback system forms between them.

The people in the middle—those at level 3, or G3 personalities—can adapt to either side of the scale to form a balanced feedback system with partners elsewhere on the scale. But even the G3 personalities have challenges because of the stubbornness of a "follower," as we'll discover in chapter 7.

According to the first principle, a lasting romantic relationship requires a balanced management system between the two partners. Ideally, for both partners to be happy, the management system should simultaneously limit selfishness and promote selflessness in both parties. The ideal of a completely balanced system may not be possible in romantic relationships where both individuals have opposite personalities (a G1 and a G5 getting married, for example). In the real world, striving for a system that is somewhat balanced is a more realistic goal.

As we can see, the fourth principle (the opposite ways of giving and receiving) is closely tied to the first (selfishness and selflessness). The two principles are related and together explain the importance of balanced systems for all human relationships or management systems. In fact, these two principles are so closely intertwined, they began as a single principle in the earliest stages of my theory. The two opposite ways of giving and receiving both have their unique selfish and unselfish aspects, and therefore, each of us has both selfish and unselfish sides at the same time.

To build a long-lasting romantic relationship, two keys are required by principle 4:

- Identify the personality (G1 through G5) of the two people in love to understand the relationship's potential. If you are dating, this will help you make the best choice early on for a long-term relationship.
- If you discover you and your partner have opposite personalities but decide to pursue the relationship anyway, you should each create a set of rules, as required by the first principle, and learn to accept each other's personalities. Your mutual project should be to work toward a middle point or learn how to live with the difference and form a feedback system that is as close to being balanced as possible.

Questions 1 through 18 in chapter 11's questionnaire will help you evaluate your personalities regarding how you give and receive love. If you are both blending types, you will have a positive feedback system that will easily last for a long time; if you are both independent types, you will have a balanced feedback system; and if either of you is at level 3, the relationship should also work.

Couples that stay together *unhappily* are the couples with at least one partner close to the middle yet on the opposite side from the other. These relationships have the potential to work out, or they are not bad enough to quit. At the same time, it is difficult for the two individuals to be truly happy without addressing the key difference in their personalities.

Sadly, from my observations, if two spouses are at opposite ends of the continuum, the marriage usually doesn't last. This theory should be helpful to you in the sense that you will know what you're up against: if you are at the opposite side of the spectrum from each other (or very close to it), you will naturally have a negative feedback system. Depending on how strong that system is, you may or may not be able to overcome it.

If you are in an existing romantic relationship that's suffering from a negative feedback system like the one just described, don't give up before following the 4-Step Method outlined in chapter 7. In following these steps, you will be able to identify the most important action items and rules, learn to truly accept each other's opposite personalities, and even be happy with them. Even though the negative feedback system is strong, you have a love history and quite possibly children as well.

For people in new romantic relationships, if you and your partner are at the opposite ends of the five-point scale (G1 and G5), you should stop here. The strong negative feedback system will make the relationship very difficult to work out in the long term. More importantly, any children you bring into the relationship will very likely have difficulty dealing with at least one of the parents. Even if one of you is at the opposite end of the G1–G5 scale and the other is closer to the center, be forewarned: that road ahead will be difficult. Make your decision accordingly.

Based on my research and experience as of this writing of where the two partners fall on the G1–G5 continuum, I propose the following red, yellow, or green lights for relationships.

Red Light

- Both people are at opposite ends of the range (one at G1 and the other at G5).

Yellow Lights

- At least one person is at the middle level (G3) (G1 and G3, G2 and G3, G3 and G3, G3 and G4, or G3 and G5).
- Both people are on opposite sides of the center (G3), but only one at G1 or G5 (G1 and G4, G2 and G4, or G2 and G5).

Green Lights

- Both people are on the same side of center (G3), either both on the blending side (G1 and G1, G1 and G2, or G2 and G2) or both on the independent side (G4 and G4, G4 and G5, or G5 and G5).

Remember, it is important to not try to move a person from one side to the other. Do not force your partner or your children to change sides. It goes against the individual's nature, and the change will not last. More importantly, it may destroy that person's self-confidence as switching from one side to the other requires giving up one's own strength and focusing only on the weakness of one's natural side, which is very inefficient.

First, accept your own side. Then, learn to accept the other side more completely. Only after you have done both of these things should you attempt to make some adjustments toward a middle point where you can meet each other and form a balanced system.

Interestingly, many leaders have G1 or G5 personalities. The more centrist G3 personalities are more balanced and can work with either G1 or G5 people. They are mostly followers since either way is acceptable to them over time. Thus, we can begin to see how the personality types defined in this chapter may determine the role of each person in a love relationship.

When a romantic relationship starts, a relationship management system automatically begins between the two people as well. This relationship management system has the personality of the dominant party. When both partners are on the same side of the G1–G5 scale, the relationship management system tends to reflect the personality of the person who is closer to one end or the other. Thus, if both partners are on the same side of the G1–G5 scale but one is at either G1 or G5, that person will be the dominant personality of the relationship system for the couple. The other personality becomes a "minority interest" and could potentially be ignored or become depressed, causing an imbalance in the relationship.

THE THEORY OF TRUE LOVE

In order to understand why a negative feedback system between two partners with opposite personalities makes long-term relationships so challenging, let's examine some examples.

If you are the blending-type person or have the self-sacrificing personality, imagine you have asked your loved one for help at least three times, and the answer was always no. Would you continue to ask for help? If you ask your partner for intimacy (sexual or otherwise) and your partner always refuses, what would you do next? Most people stop taking the initiative after a few negative responses or rejections. When you get turned down every time, it becomes challenging to remain constantly available to help others and make self-sacrifices for your partner whenever asked.

If you are at G5 and were raised to always make sacrifices for others but never learned how to get help from others, you would become vulnerable to being taken advantage of, and you may have very low self-confidence since you easily make sacrifices just to please others—even when they do not respect you in return.

If you are at G1, you are someone who never makes sacrifices for others and only gives when you want to give. You never inconvenience yourself to help others, so how would you know that others are inconveniencing themselves to help you? You most likely assume that the help you get from others never inconveniences them just as any help you offer doesn't inconvenience you. If you were at G1 as a child, perhaps you always got whatever you wanted, never needing to inconvenience yourself for others. At least one of your parents indulged you at every turn. Almost anyone raised in this way would grow up as an unbalanced person who does not know how to live in harmony with others.

Therefore, if you are at G1, you help others only when you want to and expect others to do the same thing. You do not have any expectation that others will make sacrifices for you. If you ask for help and your partner says no, you have no complaint; you see this as perfectly normal. The next time you ask, you receive a no again but with no bad feelings. You will never complain to your loved one about this because you often say no yourself if saying yes would inconvenience you.

On the other end of this continuum, some people at G5 learn from experience to lower their expectations for receiving. This strategy protects them from hurt feelings, and for many, it aligns with their religious beliefs of giving selflessly and without any expectation of reciprocity so as to accumulate "credit" for and secure the desired afterlife. When people are forced to behave in this way against their nature, it quickly diminishes their self-confidence.

To be a balanced person, the giving and receiving should match each other, as the two aspects of selflessness and selfishness, respectively. We need both (giving *and* receiving, selflessness *and* selfishness) in general to achieve and maintain balance over time for all of us to survive with others. The giving and receiving might never be precisely equal for each person in every single aspect of life. But a long-lasting relationship needs to have a balance between giving and receiving for each person involved to promote both partners' selflessness and limit their selfishness, as required by principle 1.

By nature, the way people expect to receive should be the same as (or similar to) the way they give. There should be a balance between giving and receiving. Otherwise, one person's imbalance could exhaust the other partner, who will naturally try to create a balanced system. This sort of imbalance is impossible to sustain for a long time, especially if they are on opposite sides of the spectrum or, worse, when one partner is at its opposite end.

You may still feel confused, so let me try to explain it more. By definition, the acts of giving and receiving reflect selflessness and selfishness, respectively. But blending-type people and independent-type people, because they fall on opposite sides of the continuum, actually give and receive in different ways. Both personalities have selfless and selfish aspects. At the same time, these people also receive in different ways also because they fall on opposite sides of the continuum. It is only when both people in a relationship are on the same side of this number line that they can both give as well as receive naturally. If the two people in a relationship are on the opposite sides of this personality, neither of them will be able to benefit from the other partner's unselfish aspects, and both will suffer more from each other's selfish aspects. One partner or both will eventually become exhausted by the other. A relationship in which one partner is at G1 and the other is at G5 is the least efficient for promoting each other's unselfish nature.

I want to emphasize here that we should never call a person a selfish person. Nobody is a completely selfish person by nature. There are individuals who never make sacrifices for others but also never expect or require others to make sacrifices for them in return; these are G1 individuals. If these people were to give anything away, it would be completely free—without any expectation for anything in return. It is more accurate to call these individuals self-protected rather than selfish. By nature, these people are better able to survive by themselves since they are extremely good at protecting themselves. Extreme G1 people are rare, but they do exist and are often described by others as selfish. I think this is a mistake. People at G1 need proper guidance while growing up so they do not become very difficult to live with. They need help to figure out appropriate ways of sharing and being in healthy essential relationships. Being a G1 person does not mean someone has a mental issue or even that they are completely selfish. However, their personality makes them unlikely candidates for close personal relationships day after day; it is much easier for them to live alone.

I have focused first on the people at the two ends of the giving and receiving range—those at G1 or G5. This is because it's a potential deal breaker. The opposite ways G1 and G5 people give and receive love create a huge conflict in a love relationship between a G1 person and a G5 person. They quickly form a strong negative feedback system. They soon exhaust each other's energies. If they are married, both will be in daily struggle. If they have a child, that child will generally inherit one parent's (extreme) way of giving and receiving, and a conflict between the child and the opposite-side parent will be unavoidable and sometimes so difficult that they cannot happily live in the same house. This may be the key reason for some unresolvable issues and broken relationships between parents and their children.

Studying these two extreme types of people in light of principle 2—the opposite attraction—will help us understand the key reason for most relationship conflicts. Many couples are on opposite sides of the giving and receiving spectrum, but as long as they are not both at the opposite ends, it is still possible for them to work things out. Recognizing the differences in the ways they give and receive love will help them understand each other better, accept each other, and make the adjustments necessary to reach a middle point and a balanced system.

Finally, couples in which both partners are at or near G3 (the center point of this continuum) may have their giving and receiving fall on the opposite sides. The difference should not be huge. But being so close to the center can make it difficult to know with certainty which side of the center point an individual truly is. Even though these people can feel somewhat comfortable despite being naturally just off to either side of the center, it is still easier if both partners are on the same side of this personality. Interestingly, it is the second principle—opposite attraction—that often causes couples to fall in love quickly although they are on opposite sides of this continuum, and this is generally when one partner is close to G3. These relationships can still be challenging depending on where each partner falls on continuum for ways of thinking, which will be discussed in the next chapter.

Chapter 5
Ways of Thinking

Just as there are opposite ways of giving and receiving love, there are also two opposite ways of thinking: linear and nonlinear. People think in many different ways. Some people struggle mightily to learn to think in linear ways for learning and understanding, but they are perfectly "normal" people. The two opposite ways of thinking are genetically influenced, and both deserve to be respected in their own right.

Both ways of thinking have their own advantages and disadvantages. There is no need to change your genetic way of thinking to the opposite side of the continuum. Changes should be kept to a modest level. Forcing people to change their way of thinking to the opposite way of thinking is inefficient and potentially destructive, and this can lower or destroy one's confidence.

The way people think decides how they will learn and understand. Therefore, it is important to make peace with it. Acknowledging these opposite "thinking personalities" allows an individual's natural way of thinking to be studied and developed more efficiently and enables us to treat nonlinear thinking as normal and natural rather than as a problem, disease, or disorder that needs to be fixed.

Recognizing each person's way of thinking is critical for successful relationships as well because the way we think determines our ability to understand other people, especially those with whom we are in a relationship. As with the number line for giving and receiving, a similar number line exists for how individuals think. On the thinking (or *T*) continuum, completely linear thinking is at the left end (T1), and completely nonlinear thinking is at the opposite end (T5). Any individual's way of thinking will fall naturally at some point between these two opposite ends. This can be hard to quantify with precise accuracy, but we can place any individual somewhere along the T1–T5 scale. Not surprisingly, most people have mix of both linear thinking and nonlinear thinking; people at or near the two ends are rare, but they do exist and are likely very talented in some unique ways.

The way one thinks determines how a person gains knowledge of the world. The opposite ways of thinking explain why it is easier for some people to learn math, physics, or chemistry while others excel at languages, art, music, and so on. The current educational system in the United States was developed to favor linear thinking for learning. As I've mentioned, I believe this has led to the mislabeling of students who think in nonlinear ways as having ADD or ADHD.

In this chapter, I focus mainly on how the opposite ways of thinking affect relationships. As before, I will simplify matters by using a straight line to define the continuum from 100 percent linear thinking (T1) to 100 percent nonlinear thinking (T5), so we can apply this understanding to relationships. As with the other continuums in this theory, a person's exact location on the thinking continuum is less important for relationship success than which side of the middle point (T3) each partner is on. Besides the two ends (T1 and T5), this continuum also has two sides (T2 and T4) and a center point (T3). Definitions for each of the five points along this line are as follows:

- T1: People at T1, the linear-thinking end of this continuum, almost always think in strictly linear ways; they get to the key points very quickly, swiftly identify relationship issues, love to discuss relationship problems, routinely have difficulty (which is sometimes severe) communicating with nonlinear thinkers, and are most commonly the leaders in solving relationship problems.
- T2: People at T2 often think in linear ways; they get to key points quickly, identify relationship issues accurately,

and can initiate some discussions of relationship problems. At times, these people have difficulty communicating with nonlinear thinkers, and at times, they can be the leader in solving relationship issues.

- T3: People who fall at T3 are equally comfortable thinking in both linear and nonlinear ways, and they can get to key points but do so slowly. They are able to understand and communicate with both linear and nonlinear thinkers; although, it may take time. These individuals do not like to initiate discussions of relationship issues.
- T4: Individuals at T4 are nonlinear thinkers who often think in nonlinear ways. They tend to collect random facts and pay attention to details, and they do not like conflicts and prefer to avoid discussing relationship issues.
- T5: Individuals who fall at T5, the nonlinear-thinking end of the range, always think in nonlinear ways and also have unique creative talents. T5 thinkers are both quick and good at making observations, identifying and following their instincts and "gut feelings," focusing on details, and collecting facts. They are good at ignoring relationship issues, prefer to avoid discussion of relationship problems, and have difficulty (sometimes extreme) communicating with some linear thinkers.

T1 and T2 people are on the left side as linear thinkers; T4 and T5 people are on the right side as nonlinear thinkers; and T3 people are in the center of the line—an equal mixture of both ways of thinking.

Based on my research and experience as of this writing of where the two partners fall on the T1–T5 continuum, I propose the following red, yellow, or green lights for relationships.

Red Light

- Two partners are on opposite sides of the continuum with one at the nonlinear end (T5) (T1 with T5 or T2 with T5). Avoid these two combinations for long-lasting relationships.

Yellow Lights

- At least one partner falls on the nonlinear side (T3 and T4, T3 and T5, T4 and T4, T4 and T5, or T5 and T5), or
- Both partners fall on the opposite sides of this personality without either at T5 (T1 and T4 or T2 and T4).

Green Lights

- One partner is on the linear-thinking side, with the other partner in the middle (T1 with T3 or T2 with T3), or
- Both partners are on the same side of the center point, but neither of them is at T5 (T1 and T1, T1 and T2, T2 and T2, or T4 and T4). These scores make it easy to communicate issues in ways necessary for a long-term romantic relationship.

Unfortunately, in the area of communication for the relationship and their issues, linear thinkers are at an advantage. The closer to the nonlinear end a person falls, the harder it will be for them to discuss relationship issues, especially when there is a conflict.

For relationships in which both principles 4 and principle 6 give green lights, there is not much need for expert communication skills between the partners as long as they live together. They both receive what they need from the other person by giving naturally what they can give. Therefore, even without proper communication, a balanced feedback system for their relationship comes naturally, and the relationship may last a long time. Even these couples, though, could experience problems in co-parenting. For example, if a child has a T5 personality, this could cause problems when the parents need to communicate with the child about a difficult issue. However, since the child's thinking personality is inherited from one or the other parent, biological children of parents who are not at T5 are unlikely to be at T5 themselves.

Also, if you find that you and your partner are happy when you're together but have big issues when you're not in the same place (for example, if someone frequently travels for work, or temporarily relocates to care for a family member), you are on the opposite sides of the thinking line. This makes you unable to communicate your love to each other remotely even though both principle 4 and principle 6 indicated green lights.

If principle 4 and principle 6 both yield red lights, there is no need to pursue a long-term romantic relationship. No matter how good both partners' communication skills may be, neither will be able to receive what they need from the other person in the relationship over time even if the initial attraction is strong. By their very nature, these will be short-lived relationships.

When two people from the opposite ends of the thinking line (T1 and T5) attempt a romantic relationship, communication between the couple is very difficult, if not impossible, most of the time. The partner at the linear-thinking end (T1) will always try to explain their thoughts and reasoning, which normally works with other people. However, this strategy is a complete waste of time with a partner at the nonlinear-thinking end (T5) since it will make that individual more confused about why their partner (T1) keeps repeating nonessential information while ignoring the aspects of the conflict the second (T5) partner finds most meaningful. The harder the linear thinker tries to communicate, the more frustration both parties will feel, especially when it is critical they understand each other.

As always, there is no "better" side of the continuum; both have their unique strengths and weaknesses. The linear thinkers are more likely the leaders in a relationship as far as initiating and solving relationship problems go. But they may think too quickly and act or react too strongly. The individuals who think in more nonlinear ways are more passive in solving relationship problems, but they worry less and find it easier to set an issue aside until cooler heads prevail.

Finally, as previously explained, never try to get people to change sides. Doing so goes against their nature and weakens them, and it cannot be sustained over time.

So far, we have defined and explained the two most important sets of opposite personalities for relationships of any kind (giving/receiving and thinking/communicating, as represented by the giving or *G* continuum and the thinking or *T* continuum). Now let's look at some interesting combinations of these two sets of personalities within an individual. This will be one direction I take my research in the future—studying various combinations of personalities to learn more about their relationships and individual talents. My analyses below may not be correct and will need further research, but they serve as an interesting starting point.

An individual who is G1 and T1 personality can be the strongest leader for a country but can also pose the greatest dangers to the world. These individuals' determination is unshakable because of their extremely independent personality. They can easily convince people to follow them because of their convincing communication skills. If their beliefs help the broader global community, they are great leaders. But if their beliefs are misguided or their intentions malicious, they can be destructive.

Individuals at G1 and T2, T3, or T4 are less powerful but also less destructive.

It is nearly impossible for individuals at both G1 and T5 to be powerful leaders because of their nonlinear thinking and difficulty communicating. However, people with this combination could be geniuses at inventing innovative products and systems. They have no trouble focusing intently on developing their own talent. They might also be lonely or considered narcissistic or selfish, especially if they were not raised with proper rules and guidance.

In contrast to someone at G1 and T5, someone at G5 and T1 can be a powerful national leader who is unlikely to be destructive (due to the G5 score); however, such individuals are unlikely to last very long in this role due to the exhausting nature of passionately doing the right thing for so many different constituencies over time. Then again, these G5-T1 people might not want to lead a nation in the first place as they have little (or no) desire for power.

People at G5 with T1, T2, T3, or T4 are often heroes. They are extremely giving, other-oriented people with an ability to understand and communicate effectively with a wide range of other people.

When we look at personalities and parenting, we find the following. Individuals at G4 and T2 make very good parents. Individuals at

G5 or G4 and T1 can also be very good parents as far as setting clear, consistent boundaries while being loving and supportive, but these parents are less attentive to the details of raising children. Parents at G1 or G2 might be too "strong" (perceived as blunt, cold, or uncaring) to their children, and parents at G1 and T1 could even be frightening to their children or at least aloof or emotionally distanced from them. Lastly, parents at G3 and T3, T4, or T5 may struggle or be unable to establish and enforce the rules, boundaries, and expectations successful childrearing requires. Parents who are even slightly off the center points of G3 and T3 will fare better than those at exactly the center of the continuum (G3 or T3).

Looking beyond presidents and parenting, these personalities also influence how happy and successful individuals will be in various lines of work. Let's consider some examples.

People with the blending personality (G4 and G5) are likely to burn out quickly as lawyers either in civil or criminal law. However, their personality could serve them sufficiently well in legal professions outside the courts, and this work can be satisfying to these people, especially those who think in linear ways, who tend to like contributing to society and making a difference by doing something important or righteous.

People whose personalities fall at G1 or G2 and T1 or T2 tend to be happier as leaders rather than followers. While these people are developing their careers, they can be satisfied when led by someone at G1 with T1 or G5 with T1, especially when these leaders are experts. A person at G1 or G2 and T1 or T2 is rarely happy being led all the time, but they can work well on a team of top experts.

Individuals who fall at G3 and T2 make talented managers, coaches, or educators. Perhaps surprisingly, they can also make good engineers. They tend to be determined (at times veering toward stubbornness) and need skilled managers who understand and support them. If their early childhood is characterized by excessive conflict and a lack of guidance, they may become somewhat depressed or anxious, lack self-control or self-discipline, or become chronic procrastinators who find it difficult to start projects and even harder to finish them.

Strong team or individual competitors. Strong *team* competitors likely have their personality of G on the blending side but toward the middle and their personality of T more at the linear side. On the other hand, strong *individual* competitors likely have their personality of G more on the independent side and their personality of T more on the nonlinear side.

Once we understand how these personality types influence a person's ability to work effectively in a given role, we might find ourselves making different—and hopefully better—choices about who to support as leaders of our work group, town, or even our nation. And of course, we can use our understanding of our own personalities to make better choices in our own lives, finding work that most closely aligns with our unique strengths.

Chapter 6

The 3D Matrix for the Love Personality

When it comes to love, most people have a complex mix of emotional and physical needs. These include three distinct but related types of love: emotional intimacy and two types of physical intimacy (nonsexual and sexual). As we've learned in the preceding chapters, each individual's needs are different. For example, one person might require more emotional intimacy but very little sexual and nonsexual intimacy; another person might need less emotional intimacy, more sexual intimacy, and very little nonsexual physical intimacy; a third person might have high needs in two areas but a low need in the third; and a fourth might require all three types of intimacy in roughly equal proportions.

I refer to these three aspects of love as *emotional intimacy*, *sexual intimacy*, and *nonsexual intimacy*. Nonsexual physical intimacy includes holding hands, hugging, cuddling, snuggling together, casual loving touches, and any other pleasant physical contact that is not overtly sexual in nature or intention. This mix of "love needs" is complicated, but luckily, the match between partners does not need to be perfect. There is a wide range of needs within which a couple can adapt, even in combinations defined as yellow-light pairings. As long as principle 4 and principle 5 both give green lights, these relationships are still workable.

Women often consider emotional intimacy as a fundamental aspect of (or their basic need in) romantic love. Men are more frequently taught to be mentally strong with as little emotional need as possible. From my observations, however, by nature, both women and men need emotional love. Some women have a strong need for sex, sometimes stronger than the average man's need. Some men have a strong need for emotional intimacy, sometimes more than average women's need.

In some cultures, women are taught to have less or no sexual need. In Chinese culture, we treat women who express stronger sexual needs as "bad women." In China, calling a woman sexy was not (and may still not be) a compliment; *modest* and *conservative* are more complimentary words to describe a good candidate as a future wife. In America, *sexy* is considered a positive description for many women—or at least not as negative as it might be in China. A problem arises when individuals with varying needs for sexual intimacy belong to religious groups that view sex as being solely for the purpose of procreation rather than as a basic need within human romantic love.

In traditional Chinese medicine, both men and women who have a strong sex drive and who feel physically hot at night may be diagnosed as having a *yin* deficiency; thus, having a strong sex drive becomes associated with being abnormal. Some ancient Chinese "medical" literature offer explicit, age-based guidelines about the optimal frequency of sexual intimacy for maximizing health and longevity.

In the earlier versions of my theory, I ignored the need for sexual intimacy and mainly focused on nonsexual physical intimacy. I used to define this personality as the two opposite needs of emotional love and physical love, envisioning one straight line with strong emotional love at one end and strong physical love at the other. Gradually, I accepted the fact that some men or women are born to need more sex than others and that what traditional Chinese medicine (TCM) describes as their body heat is normal to them even though they may have more heat than average.

In my TCM practice, I saw married men and married women who had unsatisfied sexual needs because their spouse had a much lower need for sex. For a long time, coming from the Chinese tradition, I believed that their imbalance was not normal. I tried to correct their yin and yang to solve their problems. I suggested that the spouses with the stronger sex drive needed to constrain their sexual activities for their own long-term health. I believed that as they aged, those patients (who came to me for other issues) would develop health problems caused by their frequent "unconstrained" sexual activity when they were younger. It took me years to finally accept and respect the fact that how frequently one needs sex is needed is also genetically based and that it can be quite different for each person. For some people, the fact that their mix of needs for intimacy (including sexual intimacy) has not been acknowledged and respected by their partners for a long time may result in anger, mood swings, or depression.

Understanding this reality led me to replace my usual concept of a two-dimensional number line with a 3D matrix that could represent a complex mix of the three intimacies—emotional, sexual, and nonsexual—to define this third important personality for romantic relationships. Identifying this mix of needs, at least at a general level, is important.

Since the need for physical intimacy has both sexual and nonsexual aspects, we need three axes (x, y, and z) to define the complex mix of needs for emotional and physical love. Let the x-axis represent emotional needs, the y-axis represent nonsexual physical needs, and the z-axis represent sexual physical needs. We now have unlimited possibilities, which does a good job of plotting all the variables. However, it also creates a problem: it's far too difficult to discuss all these different possibilities!

Fortunately, pinpointing the *exact* mix of sexual, nonsexual, and emotional needs for an individual may not be so important. (And as we'll see shortly, this three-axis model can be simplified.) This is because people usually have a fairly wide, workable range when it comes to adapting to their partner's needs based on this personality in comparison to the other two personalities. Also, many people don't have experiences with multiple sexual partners from which to form comparisons, and some peoples' mix of needs may not be very clear even to themselves if they belong to the blending personality described by principle 4. These people are more likely to prioritize and adapt to their partner's (or partners') needs, setting their own needs aside until they can't stand it anymore, which could be years. In these cases, it often appears a person's needs suddenly changed when, in fact, the needs were there all along but were either not recognized or intentionally suppressed.

As I promised, there is a simplification for the infinite possibilities in our original three-axis model. This simplification is made possible by the fact that we do not need to identify every possible variable for each individual's unique mix of needs. To simplify matters, I use only three points for each line instead of the usual five. I use one line for each of the three types of love needed: emotional love (E), sex (S), and intimacy (I). Each line has only two end points and one middle point. These simplified continuums look like this:

- The emotional (E) continuum: little emotional need (E0), average emotional need (E1), and strong emotional need (E2).
- The sex (S) continuum: little sex need (S0), average sex need (S1), and strong sex need (S2).
- The nonsexual intimacy (I) continuum: little intimacy need (I0), average intimacy need (I1), and strong intimacy need (I2).

These three-point lines greatly reduce the number of points in our three-axis model. We now have a total of twenty-seven points ($3 \times 3 \times 3 = 27$) in the space, representing twenty-seven different combined levels for the mix of needs for emotional love and physical love (sexual and nonsexual intimacy). Assume the x-, y-, and z-axes cross at the origin point (1,1,1). The twenty-seven possible combinations are the following: (2, 2, 2), (2, 0, 2), (0, 2, 2), (2, 2, 0), (0, 0, 2), (0, 2, 0), (2, 0, 0), (0, 0, 0), (2, 2, 1), (2, 1, 2), (1, 2, 2), (2, 1, 1), (1, 2, 1), (1, 1, 2), (1, 1, 1), (0, 1, 1), (1, 0, 1), (1, 1, 0), (1, 0, 0), (0, 1, 0), (0, 0, 1), (1, 2, 0), (1, 0, 2), (0, 1, 2), (0, 2, 1), (2, 0, 1), and (2, 1, 0).

It's still a lot to discuss, but let's get started and take them one at a time.

THE THEORY OF TRUE LOVE

Definitions of the Twenty-Seven Levels for Principle 6

level 1: strong emotional, strong sex, and strong intimacy need: (2, 2, 2) or E2S2I2

level 2: strong emotional, strong sex, and average intimacy need: (2, 2, 1) or E2S2I1

level 3: strong emotional, strong sex, and little intimacy need: (2, 2, 0) or E2S2I0

level 4: strong emotional, average sex, and little intimacy need: (2, 1, 0) or E2S1I0

level 5: strong emotional, average sex, and average intimacy need: (2, 1, 1) or E2S1I1

level 6: strong emotional, average sex, and strong intimacy need: (2, 1, 2) or E2S1I2

level 7: strong emotional, little sex, and strong intimacy need: (2, 0, 2) or E2S0I2

level 8: strong emotional, little sex, and average intimacy need: (2, 0, 1) or E2S0I1

level 9: strong emotional, little sex, and little intimacy need: (2, 0, 0) or E2S0I0

level 10: average emotional, little sex, and little intimacy need: (1, 0, 0) or E1S0I0

level 11: average emotional, little sex, and average intimacy need: (1, 0, 1) or E1S0I1

level 12: average emotional, little sex, and strong intimacy need: (1, 0, 2) or E1S0I2

level 13: average emotional, average sex, and strong intimacy need: (1, 1, 2) or E1S1I2

level 14: average emotional, average sex, and average intimacy need: (1, 1, 1) or E1S1I1

level 15: average emotional, average sex, and little intimacy need: (1, 1, 0) or E1S1I0

level 16: average emotional, strong sex, and little intimacy need: (1, 2, 0) or E1S2I0

level 17: average emotional, strong sex, and average intimacy need: (1, 2, 1) or E1S2I1 level 18: average emotional, strong sex, and strong intimacy need: (1, 2, 2) or E1S2I2

level 19: little emotional, strong sex, and strong intimacy need: (0, 2, 2) or E0S2I2

level 20: little emotional, strong sex, and average intimacy need: (0, 2, 1) or E0S2I1

level 21: little emotional, strong sex, and little intimacy need: (0, 2, 0) or E0S2I0

level 22: little emotional, average sex, and little intimacy need: (0, 1, 0) or E0S1I0

level 23: little emotional, average sex, and average intimacy need: (0, 1, 1) or E0S1I1

level 24: little emotional, average sex, and strong intimacy need: (0, 1, 2) or E0S1I2

level 25: little emotional need, little sex, and strong intimacy need: (0, 0, 2) or E0S0I2

level 26: little emotional need, little sex, and average intimacy need: (0, 0, 1) or E0S0I1

level 27: little emotional, little sex, and little intimacy need: (0, 0, 0) or E0S0I0

You may have noticed that I arranged the definitions of the above levels in such a way that only one of the three aspects changes at a time and only one level is different from the one in the previous example. This makes our list of level definitions easier to apply.

Before you begin considering this personality, you should check whether you and your partner have red lights from both principle 4 and principle 5. If you have two red lights, the relationship will be too difficult to maintain over time; it has short life by nature. You should avoid pursuing this as a long-term romantic relationship even if your chemistry is very good and you have a green light on your love personality.

Fortunately, many communities now allow unmarried people the freedom to date or even live together prior to getting married, which allows couples to gain experience in how well (or how poorly) their needs match before making a lifelong commitment to each other. For these people, the detailed level definitions above may not be critical as their dating experience should shed light on the suitability of any match of these complex needs. If you are in a dating (or cohabiting) relationship, I suggest you both review the list of twenty-seven levels and identify the level that best describes each of you. Then compare your numbers for all three aspects. Ideally, your numbers will be very similar with at most a one-digit difference on only one of the three coordinates. Otherwise, you may want to reconsider your relationship.

If you are not in a relationship, you can first identify your level from the list of definitions then look for someone at the exact same level on all three coordinates or someone who is an exact match on two coordinates and no more than a single point different from you on the third. For example, if you are an E2S2I2 (level 1 in our list), your very best match would be another E2S2I2, but you could also be happy with an *E1S2I2*, E2*S1*I2, or an E2S2*I1*. This is only the first personality for you to consider in a new partner; once you pass this requirement, you also need to follow the guidance for the two sets of opposite personalities in chapters 4 and 5 to decide the requirements for your options.

For married couples who are struggling but want to improve their relationships, I suggest you each identify your own level and compare the differences. Make a note of your findings as we'll discuss what to do next in chapter 7. Even if you have a red light for this personality, there are still steps you can take that might save your marriage.

Although it might seem complicated at first glance, once you start using the definitions list, it should be very helpful for the matching process, especially when time is limited. (After all, you don't need to be on a television dating show to want to find your best life partner quickly!) If both potential partners identify their own levels and then compare their results, they will have a sense of how similar or different their needs might be, which should help them make better choices about partners for healthy long-term relationships.

The following red-, yellow-, or green-light matches look complicated, but they are important when couples have not had extensive, shared, loving experiences (of any type). The red lights for this principle are the most important ones to avoid. The yellow lights do not need to be avoided as strictly. The chemistry and "love at first sight" experienced between two people play important roles during the matchmaking process as long as you ensure there are no red lights. Once you have identified each partner's level, review the information below to be sure there are no red lights. (In chapter 11, we'll look at questions for your love personality that will assist you further in making better choices as well.)

Based on my research and experience so far, I propose the following red, yellow, or green lights for principle 6.

Red Lights

- Set 1: Both partners are opposite on all three continuums. The four possible combinations of this type are the following:
    o level 1 and level 27, or (2, 2, 2) E2S2I2 and (0, 0, 0) E0S0I0
    o level 3 and level 25, or (2, 2, 0) E2S2I0 and (0, 0, 2) E0S0I2
    o level 7 and level 21, or (2, 0, 2) E2S0I2 and (0, 2, 0) E0S2I0
    o level 9 and level 19 or (2, 0, 0) E2S0I0 and (0, 2, 2) E0S2I2

- Set 2: Both partners are opposite on two out of three continuums. There are many possible combinations; a few examples are the following:
    o level 3 and level 26, or (2, 2, 0) E2S2I0 and (0, 0, 1) E0S0I1
    o level 3 and level 24, or (2, 2, 0) E2S0I2 and (0, 1, 2) E0S1I2
    o level 3 and level 12 or (2, 2, 0) E2S0I0 and (1, 0, 2) E1S0I2

THE THEORY OF TRUE LOVE

- Set 3: Both partners are opposite on one out of the three continuums. There are many possible combinations; a few examples are the following:
  o level 3 and level 8, or (2, 2, 0) E2S2I0 and (2, 0, 1) E2S0I1
  o level 3 and level 9, or (2, 2, 0) E2S2I0 and (2, 0, 0) E2S0I0
  o level 3 and level 6, or (2, 2, 0) E2S2I0 and (2, 1, 2) E2S1I2
  o level 3 and level 18, or (2, 2, 0) E2S2I0 and (1, 2, 2) E1S2I2
  o level 3 and level 20, or (2, 2, 0) E2S2I0 and (0, 2, 1) E0S2I1
  o level 3 and level 21 or (2, 2, 0) E2S2I0 and (0, 2, 0) E0S2I0

Yellow Lights

- Set 1: Partners are next to each other on all three continuums. The two possible combinations of this type are the following:
  o level 1 and level 14, or (2, 2, 2) E2S2I2 and (1, 1, 1) E1S1I1
  o level 27 and level 14, or (0, 0, 0) E0S0I0 and (1, 1, 1) E1S1I1

- Set 2: Partners are at the same level on one continuum and next to each other on the other two continuums. There are many possible combinations; a few examples are the following:
  o level 1 and level 5, or (2, 2, 2) E2S2I2 and (2, 1, 1) E2S1I1
  o level 1 and level 17, or (2, 2, 2) E2S2I2 and (1, 2, 1) E1S2I1
  o level 1 and level 13, or (2, 2, 2) E2S2I2 and (1, 1, 2) E1S1I2

Green Lights

- Set 1: Both partners are at the same level for all twenty-seven levels. There are twenty-seven possible combinations, which include the following:
  o level 1 and level 1, or (2, 2, 2) E2S2I2 and (2, 2, 2) E2S2I2
  o level 2 and level 2, or (2, 2, 1) E2S2I1 and (2, 2, 1) E2S2I1
  o level 27 and level 27, or (0, 0, 0) E0S0I0 and (0, 0, 0) E0S0I0

- Set 2: Both partners are at the same level on two out of three continuums and are only one level away from each other on the third continuum. There are many possible combinations; a few examples are the following:
  o level 1 and level 2, or (2, 2, 2) E2S2I2 and (2, 2, 1) E2S2I1
  o level 1 and level 6, or (2, 2, 2) E2S2I2 and (2, 1, 2) E2S1I2
  o level 1 and level 18, or (2, 2, 2) E2S2I2 and (1, 2, 2) E1S2I2

Stated in the simplest way, these red, yellow, and green lights for the love personality can be defined as the following:

Red Light

- Both partners are opposite on at least one of the three continuums.

Green Lights

- Both partners are at the same level.
- Both partners are at the same level on two continuums and only one level away from each other on the third.

- Note: A conditional green light exists for people at level 14 (1, 1, 1) *and* at G3, T3; these individuals should be able to work with any other levels of this personality; although, some may be easier than others.

Yellow Lights

- Any combination not identified here as a red light or green light.

As with the other aspects of human nature we've discussed, these individual needs are genetically influenced, and therefore, no one should be forced to change from one side of a scale to another. Additionally, most people's sex drives diminish with age. We should respect our natural and unique balance of needs and try to find romantic partners with similar needs. It may be unhealthy for either side to feel continually pressured to go against their nature.

If you are in a marriage that falls into a red-light category, it will be difficult to remain (happily and faithfully) married. If it is too difficult to break up and depending on your religious or personal beliefs, you might consider an open relationship if principle 4 and principle 5 both give green lights. This way, you will stay together by being honest with each other and by allowing both of you to be true to yourselves.

Arranged marriages—in which parents or other elders select the bride and groom based largely on social, economic, or other considerations and in which the bride and groom generally have no real relationship until after they are married—strike me as inherently risky as they rarely, if ever, consider any of the types of individual personalities on which this theory of true loved is based.

Finally, it's important to remind ourselves that the need for sexual intimacy is genetically influenced and that the need for frequent sexual intimacy is not something unique to men regardless of what most contemporary societies would have us believe. For example, a man with a low need for sexual intimacy but a high need for emotional intimacy would be drawn to marriage even if he could not meet the needs of a wife with a need for more frequent sexual intimacy (or a lower need for emotional intimacy). This husband is not a "weak" man; in fact, nothing is wrong with either the husband or the wife. Our culture frequently promotes the idea that all men should want sex all the time and, conversely, that all women should want emotional or nonsexual physical intimacy more than sexual intimacy. Not only is this absurd, but these messages infiltrate our self-perception as well, often leading individuals to feel they are somehow not right for feeling the way they naturally feel. These needs are genetic, and just like other genetically influenced things (how tall we are, what color our eyes are, whether we seek risk or avoid it, and so on), we should accept our differences and find suitable matches for our true, natural selves.

CHAPTER 7

Applying the Theory of True Love to Existing Romantic Relationships

My theory of true love can be applied to any setting in which two or more people live or work together. It should help us be more productive in managing and minimizing conflicts. It may be useful for personal growth and self-confidence. It may help management systems, including political systems, to be more efficient with a clear direction toward improvement. In this chapter, I will explain the application of my theory for improving existing romantic relationships.

Principle 2, opposite attraction, explains why most true-love relationships naturally form negative feedback systems and become difficult to manage. The stronger the attraction between the two partners, the harder it may be to maintain a positive relationship, depending on how opposite the two people's personalities are, as described in chapters 4, 5, and 6.

Some romantic relationships, by nature, can only last for a short time; some can find balance with some effort; and some can work out with hard work and commitment from both sides.

In this section, we'll focus on difficult romantic relationships, especially where both parties want to stay in the relationship but have all but given up hope of ever finding happiness together. If you have been married for years but you and your spouse remain unhappy with each other, applying my theory of true love may change your life. The application of the four key steps from my theory will assist you in finding the happiness that has eluded you in the relationship.

If you and your partner are on the same side of the first two personalities and are a match based on the third personality, there should be harmony in your romantic relationship. If you are far away from each other on all three personalities, you would have most likely broken up already as the relationship would not have survived for very long. All other situations between these two combinations should benefit by applying the four key steps I describe later in this section.

If your marriage has lasted for years but with difficulty, you and your partner have at least one pair of opposite personalities. One of you is most likely close to the middle on the first two personalities. This "middle" person in the relationship is the "follower." Followers are happiest without conflict, so they avoid discussing relationship issues.

The partner who is closer to either end of the continuum for any of the first two personalities is generally the "leader" of the relationship. These people often initiate discussions for any relationship problem. The follower easily becomes discouraged and quiet and holds back, and they can be stubborn. Depending on how strong the personalities of the leader are, the follower may even become somewhat depressed. Yet these individuals have endurance because of their position in the middle range of the first two personalities. They can protect themselves for survival but with just enough resistance to cause uncomfortable situations for the leader. I think of these individuals as stubborn followers. Their unfulfilled needs may subconsciously stop stubborn followers from giving their best love to the leaders whether out of self-protection or simply a lack of confidence in the importance of their own needs and the need to be at their best for themselves and for the relationship.

On the other hand, the leaders in these relationships are frustrated by their own unfulfilled needs, and they sometimes respond by acting in ways that are overly firm or even aggressive to help "improve" their partner. The leader often uses strong words, and the follower often believes they themselves are to blame. Most of the time, the leaders are stressed due to their own issues and only in need of a listener or an outlet for blowing off steam. Sometimes the stress is indeed caused by the stubborn follower (in full or in part), but it is hard for the followers to know for sure; therefore, they generally remain followers, lacking the confidence to stand up for their own needs.

In extreme cases, these are relationships of abuse, which carry with them a different set of far more urgent concerns. I am addressing the far more common, significantly milder cases, which, while not life-threatening, are not healthy relationships to inhabit. It is those relationships that are most likely to be helped by the work described in this book.

Couples in relationships that are unhappy but livable should follow at least some of the four key steps described in this chapter. Start by taking the first step and complete the remaining steps as needed. For couples with only one pair of opposite personalities, understanding the personality difference is likely enough to solve their marital issues; I have helped some couples at this level, and it was effective. For couples with two or three sets of opposite personalities, more work will be needed. Their opposite ways of giving and receiving love and the mismatching of their complex needs of emotional and physical love makes it more difficult for them to feel loved. They may be also on the opposite sides of thinking, and the way they try to communicate only makes things worse and leads to greater frustration, discouraging continued work on the relationship.

I have helped couples of different levels. It does work! You both deserve better and can be happier. If you follow the steps, you will improve your romantic relationships. I can say this with confidence because I have experienced it myself: my theory and the 4-Step Method you'll learn about in this chapter helped my own marriage. Let me tell you how.

My husband and I got married in 2002. Since then, we have seriously discussed divorce at least five times. At one point, we separated for months and tried to move forward with a divorce. But we managed to survive the period of separation and got back together with the guidance of my love theory. I gradually learned to apply my theory to improve my own relationship.

Like many other married couples, my husband and I have a deep love for each other. However, because of our opposite personalities, we were both unhappy—especially me. Sometimes I felt tightness in my chest because of the lack of intimacy that my body needed.

If I had my complete theory much earlier, things would have been different. For years, I only had the idea of opposite ways of giving and receiving to guide me. I explained this theory to my husband a number of times. I told him my daughter and I are at the two opposite ends of this spectrum, and therefore, if she and I were (hypothetically) two partners in a romantic relationship, there would be no chance, or it would be too difficult and inefficient. Yet if we put in a great effort, my husband and I could work things out because we are not at completely opposite ends of the spectrum. I tried and tried to have discussions with him, which did little to solve our problems when it came to the most important unmet needs, but it was just enough for us to keep going.

After identifying principles 5 and 6, I finished this book as quickly as I could so my husband could understand me better. I believed having him read my book would convey my theory much more clearly than I had been able to in our conversations. Reading my initial draft did help my husband understand me.

Next, I decided to improve my marriage even more by applying my theory more strictly in a step-by-step way. After I summarized the key steps, I spent two months applying them to my own marital issues. Since finishing the initial draft in August 2020, my husband and I have been working together to apply the steps that I gradually formed for my theory. We finally did it! We both are now happier with our marriage. I only wish that I had my complete theory years ago!

During those difficult years, I had the chance to help some of my patients with issues they were experiencing in their romantic relationships. I realized some of them were facing challenges similar to those my husband and I faced.

Of course, there are many reasons people stay in long-term relationships. People tend to stay married partially because of their love and partially because of their insecurities about finding a better long-term romantic partner in the future. Some stay in the relationship for financial reasons or for their children. Sometimes partners simply feel "stuck" with each other, sometimes hopelessly or with a sense of resignation. Some seek help through marriage counseling, and some try to avoid issues by burying them more deeply. If you have managed to survive together, then you should be happier with the help of this book. It will help you and your partner understand your opposite (or differing) personalities, stop unnecessary negative feelings for each other, and become certain of your love for each other.

Once I had my more complete version of the theory ready, I had the chance to use it to help six couples with their marriages. Within weeks, both partners in these marriages became much happier and had less conflict, fewer arguments, and improved moods.

Some of the couples had worked with therapists but were unable to resolve their problems. For example, one husband worked with a therapist for years and had to stop because, rather than helping improve his marriage, it made things worse by increasing the feelings of distance between the husband and his wife. In this unfortunate case, the counseling encouraged the husband to shift his focus from his marriage to his job, which only made it easier for him to ignore his marital issues.

All six couples were different, of course, but they all improved their marriages within two to three weeks. Before we look at the definition of the 4-Step Method, I like to provide you with some introduction first.

Step 1. Based on my understanding of their difficulties, I explained my theory of opposite personalities and how it might apply to their situations. I explained to them their love *for* each other should be greater than the love they actually feel *from* each other. I suggested they first *try to accept their partner's behaviors instead of taking those behaviors personally and feeling hurt*. Trying to correct the other person's personality-driven behaviors will only cause more problems. This step alone helped four of the six couples in just two weeks, and I was only working with one person in the couple! Those four couples were a good match on one of the three personalities and only differed slightly on the other two. Of course, they need to continue to work on strengthening and maintaining their new good habit.

I warned the two couples with two and three sets of opposite personalities that we might need to work on it together for months in order to see the desired result. However, one couple experienced results in just three weeks, and the other within a month. I helped these two couples work through the remaining three steps.

Step 2. Identify the two most important items each partner feels are missing from their relationship and the two most important behaviors they wish the other partner would improve. Interestingly, only one of the four people had most of the answers within an hour; the others took from one to three days. For years, they had been trying not to think about what they wanted most from each other in order to avoid disappointment.

Step 3. Consider the priorities discovered in step 2 and the two sets of rules required by principle 1 for both partners. By asking questions and listening to the individuals' answers, I helped these couples *create several rules for each partner and several items or actions for both partners to start immediately*. (Out of respect for their privacy, I won't provide the details here, but examples are given later in this chapter.)

Step 4. Implement the plan by closely monitoring to ensure both individuals follow the rules and the action lists, adjusting as necessary. We made quick adjustments to the rules and action lists as needed during the process and added two new items to one couple's original action lists.

The quick results for both couples were partially because their personalities, while on opposite sides of the continuums, were not polar opposites. Additionally, the rules and action lists were appropriate and effective, enabling each partner to see the difference right away, willingly work on their own action lists, and follow their own rules alongside their spouse. Naturally, the results for a team are different from the results when only one-half of the partnership is working.

Each couple is unique with a different personality combination on all three key principles. The rules and action lists are different for every individual. As long as both partners follow the two required set of rules established by principle 1, the process should work for all but the most mismatched couples; it's just a matter of how long it will take to see positive change and how much effort will be required.

In my experience with helping people with relationships other than romantic ones, sometimes understanding that the other person has a different way of giving and thinking is enough to help them move on from their current doubts or frustrations. As long as you understand there is an opposite way of giving and thinking, you will not take offense at other people's actions. You will stop blaming yourself and lowering your self-confidence, and you won't blame the other person and become angry or disappointed. This step alone may be enough for friendships, siblings who do not live together, and also for some work relationships.

If you are in a relationship in which you live with your partner, you need to consider what sacrifices you are currently making. If you are on the sacrificing personality side of the spectrum and the other person is not, you must learn to set boundaries so you make only those sacrifices you know you can make without seeking anything in return. Otherwise, you are creating a scenario that allows space for the other person to be selfish and take advantage of you rather than tending to your needs, and this unhealthy situation would partially be your fault. In an ideal world, no one would take advantage of anyone else, but the hard truth is that selfish people will not respect boundaries you do not enforce.

Once you set these boundaries, it is critical to learn to accept the personality differences in your relationship. First, learn to accept yourself for your own ways of giving and thinking and your own level of confidence in establishing boundaries when they are needed. Then, learn to accept the other person as they are and enjoy more of the love you have for each other. Since an opposite attraction put you two together for some reason, you will have to learn to either accept each other or live apart from each other. Do not stay in the middle, feeling trapped and without hope or happiness.

Because of principle 2 (opposite attraction) and principle 3 (the non-quantifiable nature of love), it may not be easy for people to identify what exact rules to follow and actions to take, especially for the couple with opposite ways of thinking. Sometimes this can be a very difficult process for a couple. Once you understand and apply this theory, however, you will gain clarity on whether there is real hope for improving the relationship and being happy in it or—if you discover a red light—whether you and your partner should go your separate ways.

Here is my suggestion for all couples with relationship issues:

First, apply the five love languages to your issues; these are explained in Gary Chapman's bestselling self-help book, *The Five Love Languages: How to Express Heartfelt Commitment to Your Mate*. If doing this is unsuccessful, your next step is to answer the questions in chapter 11 of this book to discover where you and your partner are in terms of the three personalities. If you discover you are not a red-light couple, you should be able to improve your relationship if you are both willing to make the effort.

The 4-Step Method will help you improve your relationship. However, the different ways you and your partner think may not allow you to communicate with each other effectively enough to follow the 4-Step Method on your own. If you discover or suspect you are in this type of relationship, a professional therapist may be helpful.

With years of practice, I have gotten quite fast at identifying the underlying keys of personality conflicts and setting up effective rules with action lists for both partners. My hope is that by explaining it to you here, your learning curve will be easier, and you will see improvements in your relationships in less time. Even my process of writing the theory down in draft form immediately helped me become more efficient and effective in all my business and personal relationships, avoiding potential conflicts and quickly finding mutually workable solutions.

Before looking at the 4-Step Method in greater detail, I'd like to offer three reminders for those of you who are struggling with true love within a difficult relationship.

- Principle 1, the selfish and unselfish aspects that exist within all of us, dictates that we all need true love. We want to give and receive love for ourselves. Yet principle 4 tells us that romantic couples mostly have opposite ways of giving and receiving love. The love between them is more difficult for each partner to feel. The true love we have for each other is always there, even during the struggles and fights, which may be frequent.

- Principle 2, the law of opposite attraction, tells us that most people entering into romantic relationships have some degree of opposite personalities. This makes it difficult to manage the relationship and requires effort from both parties. There is no way around this. And principle 3, the unquantifiable nature of love, makes it even harder to figure out the exact issues and solutions! When these challenges are further combined with principle 5, the opposite ways of thinking for communication, some situations simply become too difficult to manage well.
- Finally, understanding the red-, yellow-, and green-light situations described in chapters 4, 5, and 6 may help you reevaluate your existing romantic relationships and also make better critical decisions in the future. Even with a strong initial attraction, if a romantic couple is too opposite from each other in personality, the negative feedback system formed between them may also be too strong to overcome. Learning to identify whether a romantic relationship is sustainable for the future should be an important first step.

The 4-Step Method to develop the proper boundary for romantic relationships

Step 1. Identify the personality differences. The first thing to do is acknowledge and accept that you and your partner might have opposite personalities. To find out, both of you should answer the questions in chapter 11. These will tell you where you stand both individually and comparatively. Once you have done that, check for any red lights on each of the three personalities described in chapters 4, 5, and 6. Then, complete this first step by evaluating the viability of your relationship moving forward and make the best decision you can about your course of action. If you and your partner are close to each other on principle 6 and different but not too far from the middle on principle 4 or principle 5, this first step may be enough to help improve your relationship.

Step 2. Come up with two lists for each person. Assuming you decide to continue working through this process with your partner, you need to identify the sets of rules as well as action lists for each of you to follow. Each partner should identify the two (or at most three) most important items they want their partner to avoid doing; these will be the two rules for that partner. The rules are the boundaries you mutually agree to honor in order to respect each other's personalities. Next, create your action lists by identifying the top two (or three) actions each partner needs the other partner to take. Keep in mind that all actions must be things the partner is capable of doing. The action lists, or the to-do items, are the ways you mutually agree on to improve for each other that don't conflict with your own personality. In short, the rules are what *not* to do, and the actions are what *to* do. The rules and action lists should be adjusted depending on how things go in the third and fourth steps.

Examples of rules might include the following:

- No discussion of emotions during physical intimacy.
- No taking complaints personally, even if you feel you're being blamed.
- No "fixing" your partner's problems.
- No criticism during physical intimacy.
- No strong words.
- No over-explaining.

Examples of action-list items might include the following:

- First, hold your partner's hand, and then start talking.
- Make and maintain eye contact while talking to each other.

- Get to the key points right away.
- Listen to and acknowledge your partner without offering your opinion.
- Hold your partner's hand and reassure them you are here for them even if you disagree with their behavior.

If you do not have problems making big decisions but you do have ongoing or nonstop frustrations with each other over small matters, these examples will be of great help to you.

Step 3. Implement. Simultaneously implement the actions and follow the rules you established in step 2. Step 3 needs to be monitored through mutual, positive communication in order to make sure both partners do their best to abide by the rules and take the actions identified. This step also requires both people to learn how to love with true acceptance of their own personalities and their partner's true personalities at the same time. The third step is a learning process that will get better with practice. Learn to accept each other instead of trying to change each other. Listen to each other instead of trying to fix the other person's problems. If you cannot come to an agreement, leave it as it is. If it is too difficult to discuss issues with each other, write down the key points with less explanation; often, simply using fewer words helps clarify what's going on and what needs to happen to make things better.

Step 4. Reevaluate. Reevaluate step 3 and make changes to the current rules and action lists whenever they are needed throughout the process. This should be an ongoing process, as needed, throughout the life of the relationship.

I am often asked whether taking these 4-Step Method will help if only one partner takes them. My answer is a conditional yes: if a relationship is not too deeply troubled and if the partner going through the steps is the leader in the relationship, the process can work; more difficult relationships require both partners to follow the four-step process together.

If following the 4-Step Method does not work the first time, go back to step 2 and try again with different rules and action lists, keeping in mind that the rules should be specific and carefully chosen in order to allow each other to be true to their own personalities. Similarly, the action lists need to have *reasonable* expectations of improvement for each partner. Because the rules and the action lists are very limited (just two items each), give them serious thought and choose them wisely. All items must be both finite and fair—no laundry lists of complaints or vaguely stated wish lists. Together, the rules and action lists help us take small but measurable steps to gradually form new habits while allowing us to keep our natural personality and self-confidence. They help us improve on our weaknesses while protecting our strengths.

Proper communication is key to the implementation of the 4-Step Method. If you have opposite ways of thinking and also have trouble communicating, seek out a professional therapist who can assist you in this process. If the negative feedback system is still too negative after both partners have invested significant effort applying the four key steps, then both partners should reevaluate the relationship and decide about its future.

Over the past twenty years, I have worked with many individuals (most of whom were patients in my acupuncture practice) and some couples as well. All these people loved their partners without doubt and wanted to stay in their marriages even with incompatible personalities. This incompatibility was often in the area of the need for sexual intimacy, where one partner needed significantly more sexual intimacy than the other. Some of these couples decided to have an open marriage where the partner who needed more sexual intimacy was free to seek sexual partners outside the marriage. I understood and supported their idea based on their situations. This worked for two couples, and others ended in divorce within a few years.

There was one special couple that I would advise differently today than I did at the time. In this case, the husband's need for sexual intimacy was far lower than the wife's need. The wife ended up having ongoing relationships with other men for a period of about five years. The husband and wife never officially discussed open marriage; the wife reported that her husband was okay with her having other relationships, but the wife herself did not feel right about it. At one point, she considered divorce. When she asked my opinion on this, I strongly supported the idea of divorce as we both thought the husband deserved a better marriage. They were divorced soon afterward.

A couple of years later, the ex-husband found a girlfriend and got married. We both were happy for him. The ex-wife is still my patient and has remained single, enjoying the freedom of dating different men. It wasn't until recently that she told me she regretted the divorce for many reasons, including for the sake of their children, who were still in high school at the time. Her daughter confided in her that the stepmom flirted with other men even when the family was out in a restaurant for a family dinner, making the dad and both children uncomfortable. The daughter wondered whether the stepmom had ongoing relationships with other men without the dad's knowledge or consent.

My patient and her ex-husband had mostly green lights based on my theory now, but one aspect of the love personality (sex need) was opposite. With two children together, would it have been better to have an open marriage (with both spouse's knowledge and support) rather than getting divorced? If I had my theory then, I would have suggested that my patient and her husband speak openly about her needs and her proposal of an open marriage; this would have allowed the husband a choice in the matter (albeit a difficult one: either stay in an open marriage or get divorced) and also would have assuaged the wife's guilt about what were, in fact, extramarital affairs. It is never one spouse's place to assume divorce is the best choice for the other spouse. The husband is now in a second marriage that sounds troublingly reminiscent of the first. The husband blames himself and his naturally low need for sexual intimacy, and this, in turn, leads him to put up with his second wife's disrespectful behaviors—not only to him but to his children, and not only behind their backs but in front of their faces in public.

The lessons here are twofold: In a new romantic relationship, an opposite need for sexual intimacy is a strong red light. This is a relationship you should not pursue. In an existing marriage or similar relationship, if the other two aspects of the three-dimensional love personality are not red lights and the personalities for ways of giving and ways of thinking are both green lights, I believe the couple should at least discuss and consider a true open marriage.

Working with other couples, I have observed that many people in marriages with ongoing struggles love each other but have some personality differences coupled with inefficient ways of communicating. Often, the love personalities of the partners in these relationships have one or two yellow lights, and the ways of giving and thinking are just slightly off the midpoint and on opposite sides for both partners. These love relationships become more painful for the partner who constantly tries to find solutions while the other side is also unsatisfied as a stubborn follower, unwilling to make more effort. Before my theory was completely developed, I was limited in how much I could help these couples solve their problems. It is now clear to me that most of these couples had one person as the stubborn follower (or determined follower), and none of the individuals in these couples had a personality at the extreme end of any continuum. This tended to create couples that could stay together somewhat unhappily for years.

The determined followers like stability. They may prefer not to take risks nor to make/discuss changes, only wanting to survive by staying the same. But the leaders may need the change to continue their marriages. What can such couples do? Sometimes followers need a big push, such as a discussion of open marriage (or divorce), to motivate them to increase their effort to save the relationship. With my current understanding, I urge any couple working with me to give each other six months to a year to work on improving the relationship before making any major decisions about its ultimate fate. After that period, if either or both partners are still unhappy and if this is due to the unwilling participation of the follower, the couple should consider trying an open marriage as a last chance of salvaging the relationship. This may motivate followers to take the risk and try harder together with the leaders to work with their partners in applying the theory and saving their marriage.

An open marriage, in this situation, does not mean either partner is being encouraged to seek out other relationships; it merely gives both partners the option, therefore granting each partner a sense of freedom as well as a sense of competition with outsiders for their spouse's attention. Neither partner can take the other for granted, and they may appreciate each other more and willingly work harder as a team to improve their relationship. However, as much as some determined followers might dread any change at all (seeing a therapist, changing the marriage's ground rules, or divorcing), no one is being trapped or forced to change. If this arrangement is negotiated in advance, following the rules outlined in the 4-Step Method, an open marriage might work. If it doesn't or if either partner is unwilling to give an open marriage a try, the couple should consider divorce.

Interestingly, in China, a married man can easily have romantic relationships outside the marriage. This is partly because of the historical practice of Chinese men, especially the king, having multiple wives, partly because many Chinese people are less strict in following rules, and partly because most Chinese people try harder than most Americans to compromise themselves in order to maintain their "normal" social status. If you are a Chinese man who is considering moving to the United States, you have to consider the fact that you will have *significantly* fewer opportunities for romantic relationships outside your marriage, if that was your desire!

I strongly suggest that those who want or need to have multiple romantic relationships should make this clear to their spouse or primary partner as early in the relationship as possible. Anything else is unfair, misleading, and hurtful. Discuss the idea of an open relationship and give your partner(s) an option or equal opportunity from the very beginning or at the earliest time you understand your needs yourself. Often, people don't realize their romantic needs until after they spend some time being married, and then they hesitate to say anything out of a desire to avoid hurting their spouse, arguing, or risking rejection. As long as both sides know the truth and agree with it, an open relationship will not necessarily encourage people's selfish side to grow stronger than it should be. If this topic applies to your relationship, it should be one of the key items addressed in the four-step to-do list.

Much of the world currently conceptualize marriage as a moral commitment with some legal strings attached. Some people see marriage as a relationship in which both partners more or less "own the rights to" being in an exclusive, personal, romantic partnership with the other partner for "as long as they both shall live." Is it perfect for all love relationships and truly beneficial for our children or future generations? If we were to allow more types of marriages (traditional, open, same-sex marriage, and so on), would it more accurately reflect human nature? Would it be easier for more people to follow the rules of marriage if those rules were adaptable to these individuals' personalities? Would there be a lesser sense of betrayal and fewer lies between spouses?

Until recently, marital infidelity could end a politician's career (although, some such affairs were surely the result of marriages between badly mismatched personalities). A good president will be even better in a harmonized marriage. A struggling marriage between opposite personalities may lead the same good president to make some bad personal or political choices out of self-doubt or a perceived need for self-protection.

When there has been a betrayal in a marriage, I suggest looking at both partners (not just the betrayer) to see if there is some room for necessary improvement. Can the betrayed partner do anything to meet the betrayer's unsatisfied needs without compromising their own nature? Can the betrayer do anything to meet the betrayed partner's unsatisfied needs without compromising their own nature? Finding and respecting the truth of our love needs based on our personalities for romantic relationships is as important as following the "traditional" rules, which (like ourselves) may have room to improve.

Chapter 8

Improving Parent-Child Relationships with the Theory of True Love

All the first five principles apply to relationships of any kind, but the fourth and fifth principles play especially important roles in relationships between parents and their children.

There is no matching process for the relationships between parents and their genetic children. No parents can choose their birth children. No children can choose their birth parents. We have to work with the children (and parents) we have been given.

Principle 4 concerns the opposite ways of giving and receiving. According to my theory, these are genetically influenced aspects of a person's nature; children inherit their way of giving and receiving either from their mother or from their father. Naturally, this means some children will have a way of giving and receiving that is opposite their mother's or their father's. During the child's growth process, this makes it difficult for the "opposite" parent and child to naturally accept each other. The bigger the difference between the child and this parent, the more difficult it is for them to feel love from the other. This is especially difficult for the children, who need to feel love and acceptance from their opposite parent in order to thrive as they develop. If the parent and child are at the opposite ends of principle 4, the parent-child conflict may worsen over time and eventually result in the parent and child becoming distanced or, even worse, enemies.

Principle 5 concerns the opposite ways of thinking. If a parent and child are also on opposite sides of principle 5, the communication between them generally doesn't help them understand and accept each other. This can lead to children receiving insufficient love from their parents, which creates a very unhealthy environment in which to grow. Addressing the natural conflicts caused by these personality differences is essential for the child's healthy, natural development.

These key personality differences in principle 4 and principle 5 make it challenging for some children to receive the love they need. If the parent and child are at the opposite ends of both personalities in these two principles (not just simply on opposite sides, but rather closer to the midpoint), they are more likely to be enemies. They may never be able to recover. My now-adult daughter, Janet, and I are at the opposite ends of both principles 4 and 5, and without the guidance of my true love theory, we could never be as close as we are today; we would have remained at a distance or even enemies.

Principles 4 and 5 define the two most important pairs of opposite sides of the personalities related to relationships. These personalities cannot be made to change from one end of the spectrum to the other. Children who are forced to switch sides will most likely lose some self-confidence since switching sides goes against one's nature. More importantly, there is no need to make the switch because each way of giving and receiving and each way of thinking has its own strengths and weaknesses. These personality differences are not the same as forming bad habits while growing up. They deserve our true respect as an inherited part of each individual's unique makeup. Everyone is capable of making some improvements but incapable of completely switching sides. We all need to focus on developing our strong side first and then improving on the weak. Ignoring our strengths to focus only on improving our weaknesses is not only inefficient; it can be destructive.

Identifying the two key personality types in themselves and their children will guide parents in child-rearing. This will help children grow up with more confidence by providing them with a healthier parent-child relationship, better guidance, and the love that they require.

Parents also need to implement both sets of rules required by the first principle. By encouraging the child's selfless aspect while simultaneously limiting the selfish aspect of their personalities, parents can aid children in developing their strengths and decrease any weaknesses related to their personalities.

If neither parent is good at solving relationship problems and both parents have strong personality conflicts with their child, we could try—as a community network—to see parenting as a professional service. Perhaps someday there will be a social structure in which parents in these situations could send their children to live with "professional parents" during school terms, with the children returning home to their birth parents during school vacations (or as desired). One pair of professional parents take up to eight or ten children. These children will, in effect, have two pairs of parents: their genetic parents, who have the opposite personalities, and their chosen professional parents, who do not. This gives children a better chance of growing up healthy both mentally and physically. Although this represents a nearly complete shift in our current view of parenting, it might result in fewer children suffering from the stress and depression that can result from growing up in a negative environment. Couples with personalities of G4 with T2 (a 4 on the giving continuum and a 2 on the thinking continuum) should make excellent professional parents as they can understand and communicate effectively with most children since their own personalities straddle the center point of both the giving and thinking continuums.

In my work, I have gotten to know some adults who had strong personality conflicts with one or both parents during their childhood. Without understanding the idea of opposite personalities as part of their natural personality differences, they usually felt hurt and thought their parents had never accepted or loved them. Some of them carried this negativity into their adult life, suffering from depression, anxiety, or both. Some have little trust that their own romantic relationships will be successful or that their romantic partners will truly understand or love them.

I have also noticed that if the dominant parent—the stronger of the two parents when it comes to making important decisions in a family—has giving and thinking personalities opposite from those of the child, it is easy for this parent to favor any children whose personalities match their own. The children with the opposite personalities are more likely to grow up with less confidence and more anger toward that parent (or both parents). Opposite siblings often develop strong negative feelings toward each other as well. Even with years of professional therapy, their anger remains and is difficult to resolve.

Let me reiterate this: while raising children, parents should first follow principle 1 and have both sets of rules for each child's development. If you and your child are on the same sides for both personalities, this should be easier for both of you; if you are on opposite sides for one or both personalities, it may be very difficult for both of you. Parents first need to show their love for any and all their children, including demonstrating their acceptance of personalities different from the parents' own. When there is conflict or frustration, parents should use the four-step process described in chapter 7.

Most of us learn how to be a parent through personal experiences in our own childhoods, watching and experiencing how our own parents treated and taught us. Some of these approaches might be completely wrong, but we don't know anything different and so continue to mimic our parents' modeling with our own children. Or if we did not like the ways our parents treated us, we might react by trying to do anything *but* what our parents did. Of course, this might not be the best way to parent either. I believe best practices of parenting should be taught in schools starting at a young age. As part of this curriculum, students could be taught to identify the personality differences, understand the importance of accepting the true personalities for each person, and learn how every child needs to be raised with two sets of customized rules designed for their unique personality combination. I strongly suggest that systematic research be conducted with the goal of developing a complete parenting curriculum based on this theory.

Until such trainings are developed, parents can benefit from following a few basic guidelines. First, parents should learn to identify their children's personalities and accept any naturally opposite personalities they might discover. Second, parents should follow principle 1 and set up two sets of rules for each child to encourage selflessness and limit selfishness. How easy or difficult this will be will depend on how similar or dissimilar your personalities are. If you are on the opposite side for both personalities, make sure you accept your child's personalities no matter how much conflict you may have with your child. *Your true love and full acceptance of your child's natural personalities is the key to the child's self-confidence.* Third, if there is conflict or frustration between you and one of your children, simply follow the same four-step process described in chapter 7, skipping the questions (found in chapter 11) about romantic love. Work together with each child to make rules and action lists to the extent your children can consciously participate in this. If the children are too young to participate as equals, you will need to put yourself in the child's shoes and act on their behalf. Such honest altruism is expected of any parent even when it is difficult. Do your best for your children here, as always.

In my experience with my daughter, Janet, I discovered that our most important rule was "Do not try to explain things in face-to-face discussions." In our case, these discussions—which I had hoped might be teachable moments in which I could help my daughter through some struggles—generally ended in frustration for both of us and both of us saying something hurtful to the other. At their worst, these interactions could even lead to hating the other person! You have to find some other ways to communicate properly.

One indicator that you're working with someone whose personalities are opposite from your own is that simple conversations suddenly and inexplicably become fights. These constant fights erode the sense of love between parent and child. As parents, it is your responsibility to get over the hurt feeling quickly and reassure your children that you love them *no matter what*. Next, you must find a way to help them understand that the hurtful words have nothing to do with the love between you two and, furthermore, that the disagreement did not mean one of you was right and the other was wrong; it was simply caused by the key personality differences.

Sometimes, with opposite personalities living under the same roof, fights are nearly impossible to avoid. This is why I suggest one item for your action list be this: "Forgive and forget any hurtful words we both said to each other as soon as possible and believe in the love we have for each other." Often, when people fight, they say hurtful things that do not reflect their truest feelings. Just as we often misspeak, we also often mishear or misinterpret things said during an argument. We are trying to defend and protect ourselves from a perceived threat. No matter what unfortunate things you may have said or (mis)heard, the underlying love you have is still there, and it's very important for both of you to feel it and believe in it. This process of improving is difficult but very rewarding!

Although this work can be hard, it is not without the occasional fun story. I'd like to end this chapter with one such story from my own family.

My daughter adopted two huskies about six years ago. We all love these dogs. Huskies require a lot of work from their owners and are generally considered fairly difficult dogs best suited for experienced owners. Any one of us alone would not be able to meet the needs of two huskies; keeping both dogs requires teamwork.

Because Janet and my husband, Andrew, have very different personalities, the dogs gradually became a big point of contention between them. Janet, as the established owner of the dogs, has her own strong opinions about how to raise and train our dogs, which she is entitled to; and she insisted on being strict with the dogs to ensure they behaved properly at all times. I followed Janet's rules fairly closely, and there were no issues between us. True confession: I do sometimes feed the dogs human food when they beg me for it, which is against Janet's rules. I know that Janet has the right to say no to me about this at any time, but I explained to her that it is too difficult for me to *never* spoil the dogs. And she accepted this explanation. When Janet would catch me breaking the rules, she'd remind me to at least get the dogs to sit and give a paw before I gave them a special treat. I would apologize and comply. However, Andrew is a stubborn follower (as described earlier) and, as the dogs' "grandpa," has his own strong opinions about raising dogs. In fact, his point of

THE THEORY OF TRUE LOVE

view is the opposite of Janet's: Andrew believes dogs have short lives and therefore should get to do everything they want to do and have as much fun and freedom as possible. My view was somewhere in the middle of these two diametrically opposing views.

Both Janet and Andrew prefer to avoid conflicts by not initiating discussions they suspect will be difficult. Instead, every so often, they will insist on getting their own way on some small matter regarding the dogs, especially if the other person is not present. Because I could understand the reasoning for both of their views, I felt that I had to step in as the mediator to prevent these small disagreements from possibly escalating into bigger conflicts between them. But I could never make their issues completely go away. The differing opinions relating to the dogs began creating significant distance between my daughter and my husband; they began to talk less with each other overall simply to avoid talking about dog-related topics they knew they disagreed on.

A few months ago, I decided to try to apply my theory to this unsatisfactory situation with the dogs. I followed the 4-Step Method. I talked to both my husband and my daughter separately and initiated two sets of rules for each of them based on my understanding of their issues. I monitored their progress, and whenever I noticed a problem, I sent them reminders. After only two months, I saw that their relationship had significantly improved. It felt amazing for me to see this big change as a result of the application of my theory. Andrew and I do still repeat our bad habits at times, and Janet still has to police us now and then. But the overall situation is much more positive. Finding the proper communication between two people with different personalities can be so rewarding!

CHAPTER 9

Finding the Right Romantic Match by Applying the Theory of True Love

The theory of true love can be used to evaluate new relationships right at the outset before they become serious or firmly established. By applying the theory to new relationships, you'll gain insight into what sorts of challenges the relationship might pose if you move forward with it. Regardless of what you discover—a perfect match or a potential train wreck—you'll have more confidence in your ability to see things clearly and make the right choices about the relationship's future.

Some of my patients have mentioned that, for a variety of reasons, they were unsure about their chances of finding happiness in a long-term romantic relationship. Even before this book was finished, many of these patients were excited by the theory, and quite a few were eager to get started as soon as possible. If you are at least partially convinced by my theory about the existence of true love and decide to give it a try, you should follow the ideas in this section to make your search more efficient. If you are only interested in short-term relationships and you think they are more appropriate for your personalities, you could skip this chapter, but be sure to identify your love personality as explained in chapter 6 as doing so will give you greater clarity about which partners will most likely meet your needs in short-term romantic relationships.

THE THEORY OF TRUE LOVE

To find the best match for a long-term romantic relationship, follow these steps:

1. Identify your personality levels for all three personalities by answering questions in tables 11.1, 11.2, and 11.3 and following the instructions in chapter 11. If you need my help, please go to my website: http://thetheoryoftruelove.com, and follow the instructions or email your answers of all the questions in chapter 11 to yaping@thetheoryoftruelove.com.
2. Write down the personality levels and some traits that you would like your long-term romantic partner to have and the personality levels and some traits that you would like to avoid in your partner.
3. Start dating either through dating websites or the traditional way.
4. Once you have found someone you like who is also curious about trying for a long-term romantic relationship, ask your potential partner to identify their personality levels by following the first step in this list.
5. Compare your personality levels to those of your new love interest, following these guidelines for matches:
    a. Start by comparing your love personality (explained in chapter 6). If you discover a red light, stop. The two of you should either break up or decide to remain friends only. If you don't get a red light when comparing your love personalities, proceed to the next step.
    b. Next, start comparing your answers for the other two personalities described in chapter 4 (ways of giving and receiving) and chapter 5 (ways of thinking).
        i. *If your answers yield two red lights (for both personalities being opposite), stop.* You have to start with a better match. Not only do these red lights indicate the romantic relationship is unlikely to last, they also make it likely that any children you might eventually have together will have red lights with

at least one of you as parents. This is a very challenging situation best avoided at the outset.

ii. *If your answers yield one red light (you and your partner are opposite on one of these two personalities), also stop.* These red-light differences would still be too difficult for a long-term relationship, and you still have the chance to try for a more compatible match. Finding a match without any red lights will create a positive or balanced feedback system within the relationship, which will encourage both sides to give more and become more confident; this will be more efficient for your daily life.

iii. *If both personalities yield green lights, you are very lucky!* Go ahead with this relationship with confidence that it should work well naturally without much effort.

iv. *If your comparison of all three personalities yields one or two yellow lights but no red lights, you should stay in the relationship*, but you may need to follow the 4-Step Method detailed in chapter 7 when issues arise.

v. *If your comparison of all three personalities yields three yellow lights, I suggest you move on unless you have a very strong attraction to each other.* These relationships require an inordinate amount of effort from both partners, but if your attraction to each other is very powerful, there is a chance you will be able to find balance and maintain a successful long-term relationship.

You have now done your best to understand yourself and your partner. You have compared your personalities, needs, strengths, and weaknesses and considered the relationship's future potential for mutual happiness or strife. You have made an informed decision. You are prepared for the conflicts you may have in the future that are caused by personality differences. With the 4-Step Method described in chapter 7, you should have the ability to work out a long-lasting romantic relationship.

Because of the law of opposites attracting, most relationships eventually face challenges of some sort. Given human complexity, this is natural. Believing in the true love you and your partner have for each other and following the 4-Step Method closely will help you get through these expected challenges and find lasting harmony in your love relationship.

From my observation, most people choose a long-term romantic partner who is somewhat different from themselves; this is the law of opposite attraction. We do not seek copies of ourselves even though these personalities might work out with little effort. Interestingly, couples in which the partners are on opposite sides of the midpoint but with one person closer to that midpoint are most common. The difficulty is in identifying which side of the midpoint people are on and if they fall just off to one side or the other. If this position is misidentified, a green light can change to yellow. If this happens and you and your partner have a strong attraction to each other, follow the 4-Step Method in chapter 7, and you should be fine. The process may be difficult, but it will be worth your effort.

As I mentioned earlier, we find an interesting situation when it comes to two romantic partners with blending personalities. These people are less likely to fall in love with each other and begin a positive romantic relationship. The blending personalities are "softer" and far less likely than independent personalities to seek out a romantic partner and initiate a romantic relationship. Once in a relationship, the blending personality traits limit these individuals' chances to maintain their relationship over time. Two blending personalities, being similar, will not feel a strong pull of the law of opposite attraction at the beginning of the relationship. But even before that, neither of these individuals is likely to be proactively pursuing new romantic relationships; both will be waiting for someone else to make the first move. For that to happen, they need someone with an independent personality. Third, blending personalities are not strong in identifying and protecting what they really want since they are more open to putting the other's needs first. These are just three of many factors that could stop two blending personalities from becoming (or remaining) a romantic pair. If you are a blending type and you know that a new potential relationship might lack the natural attraction between opposites, I suggest going ahead and giving it a try without worrying about rejection. Even if one of you has doubts, give it a try to see what may happen. Two blending personalities naturally should form a positive feedback system that will easily last forever once you two are in love. If you two are lucky enough to fall in love with each other, then you will believe in true love and be stronger and better able to protect your romantic relationship against any other negative factors!

I have a feeling that if those popular dating shows on TV were to apply my theory, the results would be more positive for both partners (although maybe not for the show's ratings!) and also provide a larger positive influence on viewers.

Now let's look at some examples of results you might find and what those results imply for a relationship's future.

If two people are on opposite sides of the midpoint on principles 4 and 5, their love relationship is almost certain to form a negative feedback system. The initial love attraction may be strong, but sooner or later, the selfish side will take over, and the partners will become unable to encourage the other's unselfish side. Principle 5 dictates that their ways of thinking will prevent them from properly communicating their opposing, unsatisfied needs. There is love between these partners, but it is too difficult to feel. Therefore, their unavoidable conflicts and unsatisfied needs will continue to grow over time. This love relationship is inefficient and too negative for both partners. It would be better to leave each other alone and avoid becoming enemies.

In contrast, if a love relationship has green lights on all three principles (4, 5, and 6), the love relationship forms a positive feedback system. It should last for as long as both partners want it to, and in fact, it may be very difficult to break up.

Romantic relationships with two green lights, not surprisingly, can go either way: some will form a balanced feedback system, which can last for as long as you choose without much effort, others will work out with proper effort, and others are best avoided.

Now let's look at what specific red-light/green-light combinations might mean for your relationships.

- If you get a *green light only on principle 4 and principle 5*, you should be good friends rather than in a long-term romantic relationship.
- If you get a *green light only on principle 4 and principle 6*, it should not be too difficult to establish a positive or balanced system even without proper communication. Both partners should be able to receive what they need from each other as long as they are living together. However, there are two important warnings for people in these relationships:
  o Try not to live apart for extended periods of time because a long-distance relationship requires more communication, which does not occur naturally between these two partners.
  o It is better not to have children in this circumstance since parenting requires a lot of communication, which you most likely won't be able to handle. If you do have children, you may need occasional help from a professional therapist to reach a workable middle ground or make decisions when you and your partner have different opinions about how to raise your children.
- If you get a *green light only on principle 5 and principle 6*, the relationship might still work with the help of this theory. Know that it may be a difficult journey for you both to change your negative feedback system into balanced one. When help is needed, follow the four key steps in chapter 7.
- If your results show *red lights on all three principles (4, 5, and 6)*, stop trying to have a romantic long-term relationship with this partner. Save whatever good feelings you have toward each other and say goodbye no matter how strong the initial love attraction may have been. Relationships of

this type are simply too difficult to work out. The chance of falling in love is rare for a couple with all three red lights, but if this is your situation, you should end the relationship as soon as possible.

- If you get a *green light only on principle 6,* enjoy the short excitement. There is no chance for a long-term romantic relationship.
- If there's a *green light only on principle 4 or principle 5 (but not on both),* it's better to keep the relationship platonic. Two or three green lights are necessary for a successful long-term romantic relationship.
- In any of the compatible scenarios above, *if you switch one or two green lights to yellow,* the relationships are still workable but could be very difficult and will require consistent hard work from both partners. Make a wise decision early to avoid unnecessary struggles in the future. If you do want to give the relationship a try, proceed with caution and be prepared to accept a departure at any time. You will need this book as guidance.
- If *all three lights are yellow,* I strongly recommend avoiding a long-term romantic relationship.

CHAPTER 10

Applying the Theory of True Love to Other Areas of Life

Once you understand the theory of true love and how it works, you'll probably begin to see its applicability in many diverse settings outside your personal life. In this chapter, we'll look at some examples of how the theory may be applied in other types of relationships and systems. This is a brainstorming discussion of possible applications of the theory; these initial thoughts are intended to spark creative thinking and conversations about ways the theory might help us improve some imperfect aspects of modern life. These are musings, not proposals, and this is not an exhaustive list but merely a sampling. Some of the ideas may prove impossible to implement, or they may create unforeseen new problems. But there's no harm in considering whether (and how) the theory might help improve societal relationships as well as personal ones. Experts in the respective fields can assess each application's value.

Family law

In the United States, current laws regarding marriage, divorce, child support, and alimony were set in place to protect the interests of non-wage-earning spouses (traditionally, stay-at-home moms) and place a real, financial value on the contributions they made to the family and household. However, in some cases, these laws can inadvertently encourage selfishness on the part of the non-wage-earning spouse when that spouse (perhaps motivated by anger, resentment, or vindictiveness) is determined to take everything possible from the wage-earning spouse in the divorce decree. These laws, expressed through the divorce decree and detailing each person's rights and obligations to the other after the divorce, can also discourage the non-wage-earning partner from becoming financially independent. These laws were established through long, hard battles mostly on behalf of women, and they provide essential financial recognition and protections to non- or lower-wage-earning spouses when marriages collapse. But there is room for manipulation and, therefore, room for improvement. The system would be fairer and less vulnerable to manipulation if the laws did more to encourage unselfish behavior and discourage selfish behavior for both parties.

The workers' compensation system

The workers' compensation system in the United States (basically) only allows the lawyer representing the injured worker to be paid from the settlement of a workers' compensation case. The system is not set up to pay lawyers for convincing health insurance companies to pay the injured workers' medical bills in the absence of a workers' compensation court case. These unpaid medical bills are the primary reason injured workers file workers' compensation claims, and many of the people filing those cases would rather *not* file one if only they could get the medical bills related to their workplace injury paid by their insurance company.

Workers' compensation cases can only be filed when a worker has suffered a long-term disability caused by a workplace injury. There is no role for a workers' compensation attorney in the workers' earlier efforts to get the bills paid through the regular channels. Very often, the lawyer gets paid a set percentage (often established by the courts for all such cases) of the settlement amount, which encourages lawyers to take on the most egregious cases that they think will end in the largest settlements for their client (the patient/plaintiff) and the biggest payout for themselves. These laws were established to protect the individual employee who gets injured on the job, especially when the injured party works for a big, rich, powerful company. However, as with the laws for divorce, workers' compensation laws also leave room for manipulation—not only by workers making fraudulent claims but by workers' compensation lawyers trying to take on large employers for the biggest settlement they can get. This complex situation should be revisited with the idea of encouraging selflessness and discouraging selfishness—in plaintiffs, defendants, and lawyers alike.

Political systems of the United States and China

In the United States, the political system focuses on limiting people's selfishness and protecting individual rights. However, it is weaker in promoting people's unselfish side, and it emphasizes respecting each person's needs over the needs of the larger society. This makes it harder for the United States to request personal sacrifices from the people living there. A prime example of this situation is how hard it was to get everyone in the United States to comply with simple, proven public-health guidelines (wearing a mask, washing hands, and maintaining an appropriate distance from others) during the COVID-19 pandemic. This is the opposite of China's political system, which emphasizes self-sacrifice from all people and enabled a quick response to limit the spread of the novel coronavirus. Yet China's system is weaker than the United States when it comes to limiting people's selfishness. Steve Jobs would not have been nearly as successful if he lived in China.

Without either the Chinese or the United States' political system, I would not have my theory today.

Chinese Confucianism and communism together taught me to always try my best to put my country at first, the group or others second, and myself last. I tried to do this, but it was hard, especially when I was in deep struggle during my first marriage and felt my sacrifices for my marriage were not properly understood or rewarded. Believing in the righteousness of making sacrifices led me to search diligently to understand the truth of love for myself. It led me to discover my initial love theory. Living in the United States allowed me to divorce my ex-husband and live the life of my choice instead of the life I was raised (in China) to believe I was supposed to live: a life seen through others' eyes, focused on the needs of the group or the country. In the United States, I became able to understand the truth of myself and the truth of the opposite personality types, and I completed this theory. The theory is only possible because I have spent my life in two opposite political systems.

Thousands of years ago, teaching based on the work of Chinese philosopher and politician Confucius (551–479 BCE) focused on promoting a person's unselfish side. It assumed that everyone could be taught to make self-sacrifices, even those who might naturally be at the extreme end of the independent personality in my theory, who would surely struggle to do so.

Believing people are naturally inclined to make sacrifices was complementary to the Communist ideal; in fact, I believe this complementarity is why Communism thrived in China. But this view is one-sided and ignores the independent nature of human beings. Both Confucianism and Communism define those who make sacrifices for the common good "good people" and those who do not make such sacrifices "enemies." Therefore, in my theory, the Chinese political system represents the extreme end of the blending personality. The much younger political system in the United States, on the other hand, represents the opposite—the extreme end of the independent personality—in the sense that it emphasizes personal rights and individual independence. It empowers those with independent personalities to shine. The self-sacrifice nature was largely ignored when the US political system was established, and to this day, it remains very protective of individuals' rights.

Neither system is perfect, but the Chinese system is easier to change because it is based on the nation as a unit rather than the individual as a unit. Both political systems have their own strengths and weaknesses based on these opposite personalities. Neither country can, should, or will change from one side of this continuum to the other, but both can be improved by understanding and accepting the other "national nature" and becoming more balanced themselves. Rather than competing with each other over which country is best, they could compete to see how they can become more balanced and more attractive to citizens hoping to live a better life.

What might these changes look like? Let's take our brainstorming in that direction for a minute, starting with the United States. The US political system is very complicated, often inefficient, and difficult to change. This itself should be the first improvement project. Improving the political system should be an ongoing matter funded by government grants to advisory groups of unbiased experts and researchers (rather than industry leaders with skin in the game). These researchers could conduct research on our political systems and processes, searching for strengths, weaknesses, and opportunities for improvement. Having identified areas in need of improvement, the research teams could then work with other qualified experts to design, test, and implement solutions. These solutions might be temporary (in the case of short-lived emergencies) or permanent. While still respecting the independence of local and state governments, some solutions could be implemented nationally when it makes sense to do so (for example, laws about broad issues like climate change or public health or laws about how the government might work more efficiently and be less subject to party politics, which serve only to delay or disrupt the intended functioning of the democracy).

All former presidents and high-level leaders, especially those familiar with the US legal system, would be invited to participate in this nonpartisan group—the National Systems and Policies Improvement Department. They would be expected to produce an annual improvement proposal that includes suggestions for efficient implementation and make it publicly available free of charge.

The current state of two completely opposite political parties in the United States sometimes reminds me of my old arguments with my daughter. Sometimes it is impossible for us to agree with each other and find a common ground; we have to agree to disagree and move on. If two political parties were formed when likeminded people with similar personalities gathered together to form the Republican party on one hand and the Democratic party on the other, the two parties may never be able to find a common ground in many situations. Maybe the parties—from individual members to elected leaders—could agree to disagree, but let each side do its job without undue interference based *not* on what is best for the nation but on party affiliation and the selfish desire to be reelected. People from all political parties seem to agree that the United States has serious issues that should be improved, yet both parties continue to allow, encourage, or participate in activities intentionally designed to impede progress and perpetuate governmental inefficiency while problems fester and people suffer.

Whether my ideas are terrific or terrible, implementing them will be far more difficult and much slower in the United States even if the president agreed with them. This is because of the intentionally (constitutionally) limited power granted to the president and the significant individual rights granted to US citizens. In China, it would be a very different story: if I had a great idea and managed to convince the president of China to agree with me, change would happen very quickly. In the United States, there is more open discussion of and interference with a president's plans because there is more freedom for people to speak out against existing or proposed policies or against political leaders themselves.

On the other hand, my theory has led me to consider four key tasks that I believe could improve the Chinese system. However, in following the current political policies in China, I will not put these ideas in this book, and I will never discuss them either. Sharing these ideas with anyone other than the top leader would likely cause more harm than good for China. I understand and respect the Chinese political system, which requires us all to speak in one voice to synchronize the sacrificing energy of the people across all of China. I also believe that all Chinese political leaders want or intend to do their best for the country and its people. With my theory, the right people at the right time will figure out some great ideas for China's improvement. The key for any management system seeking to become more powerful and efficient is to find the optimal balance between promoting unselfish aspects and limiting selfish aspects for all parties while building on its own strengths and strictly limiting its key weaknesses, as defined by its own personalities.

Both the Chinese and US political systems have their advantages and disadvantages. I love both countries, and I hope both will become even better in the future, be the best examples possible of two different systems, and become more accepting of each other for a more peaceful coexistence. All political systems of the world should have laws in place to prevent their leaders from initiating frivolous conflicts or avoidable wars. This is especially true when a political leader is at G1 on the giving continuum and T1 on the thinking continuum as these individuals can be both powerful and destructive.

I am not a political scientist, but as someone who has firsthand experience living in both China and the United States for many years, I have developed some opinions about how these systems might be informed by my theory. I offer my ideas here only as preliminary thoughts, intended to spark further exploration.

China and the United States are at the two ends of the blending and independent personality line (the G continuum). Every country in the world has a unique personality of its own and lands at one spot on this straight line. Some countries are more toward one end or the other, and some are closer to the middle. They all have their own strengths and weaknesses. Following the principles of this theory—which urge us to honor every individual's unique personality and focus on keeping our strengths while improving our weaknesses—all countries should respect each other's political systems more and work together to establish or improve boundaries that would allow every country to be true to itself without harming others.

The thinking (T) personality for communication is not as critical to a country's political system as it is to individuals since the top leaders of any country will include some individuals with the thinking personality of T1 and T2. They can be leaders by incorporating opposing views and conflicting concerns for their country in international communications. In this way, the communication personality one country presents toward another country can always be as strong as it needs to be.

Just for fun, let's imagine that we will have the following three different world competitions for all countries, just like the Olympic games:

- A competition for being the most efficient country at promoting personal inventions/talents.
- A competition for being the fastest country to response to national or international emergencies.
- A competition for being the most relaxing country for people to live in.

Which country would you pick as the winner of each of these competitions?

Some of my patients have asked for my advice about whether or not they should move to China, especially in the past few years when business opportunities there became more attractive than ever before. My answer is entirely based on each patient's personality type. Based on your own personality types for giving and thinking continuums (see chapters 4 and 5), here is what I would suggest:

Generally, if you have the blending personality, especially if you are at G4 on the giving continuum, you might very well live more happily in China than in the United States. On the other hand, if you have the independent personality, especially if you are at G1 on the giving continuum and T5 on the thinking continuum, you will likely be happier living in the United States. The following are two exceptions:

- If you are at G5 on the giving continuum, T1 on the thinking continuum, and are not interested in politics or power, then living in the United States should give you more freedom.
- If you are close to G3 on the giving continuum but with an independent personality, living in China (especially growing up in China) will help you be able to adapt to people with other personalities more easily as a follower in relationships.

THE THEORY OF TRUE LOVE

Legal cases and conflict resolution

This theory could also be applied to improve many aspects of our legal system and conflict resolution here in the United States. Based on the first four principles, a legal system needs to focus both on promoting unselfishness and limiting selfishness. Because of the second principle, in many situations, the rules we are trying to enforce are somewhat unquantifiable and are therefore difficult to implement fairly, consistently, and accurately. We need to try harder to make the rules for the implementation of all laws as specific as possible. The practice of dividing felonies into classes is an example of this, but we can do more to ensure the punishments for various illegal activities are delivered without bias.

At the same time, in order to encourage selflessness, the legal winners of *frivolous* cases should not be rewarded financially in order to discourage people from filing bogus court cases. Such self-serving lawsuits do not benefit the society in the long term, and they create years-long backlogs in the courts, which keep legitimate cases from being heard. We should do whatever we can to help our legal system encourage better individual behavior for a better society in the long term. This includes conducting better screening for unsubstantiated lawsuits as well as ensuring criminals receive sentences that are neither too lenient nor too draconian.

Let's shift our focus from broad systems down to professionals and the fields in which they work.

Throughout history, political heroes are usually at level 5 of principle 4 (G5 on the giving continuum); they are sensitive to other's needs and easily make self-sacrifices. The most respected and famous political leaders, such as George Washington and Abraham Lincoln, are in this category. They both made personal sacrifices for the good of the country and its people. In contrast, the most infamous political leaders or dictators are at level 1 of principle 4 (G1 on the giving continuum); Napoleon, Hitler, and Saddam Hussein are in this group. These G1 political leaders could have moved their countries *forward* had their beliefs been aligned with their societies' needs.

Attorneys at level 5 of principle 4 (the blending end of the giving continuum) will be better at reaching a settlement in cases where conflict is best avoided. Attorneys at level 5 of principle 4 (especially those at G5 on the giving continuum) will also be most likely to burn out from their work and may not last long in this career; they are highly considerate of other people's feelings and always try their best to be fair, and their work has a major impact on their personal life. In contrast, attorneys at level 1 of principle 4 (G1 on the giving continuum) will be stronger in cases, solely focused on protecting the side they represent, not caring how it might impact the other side. These individuals are also less likely to suffer from professional burnout.

Law enforcement officers at level 5 of principle 4 (G5 on the giving continuum) are very unlikely to fire unnecessary gunshots on the job more than once and are likely to have difficulty recovering from any unnecessary discharge of a firearm. At the other end of principle 4, police officers at level 1 (G1 on the giving continuum) are more likely to follow all traffic rules and write tickets to every person who breaks a law, whereas police officers at G5 may never write a ticket, depending on the community they serve.

Of course, principle 4 (the giving continuum) isn't the only one that influences our daily lives outside of our romantic or parent-child relationships. Principle 5 (the thinking continuum) concerns how we think, learn, and communicate ideas, which naturally permeates nearly everything we do. Let's look at some interesting examples you've probably already experienced in your own life.

If you're reading a book on a topic that interests you yet find you cannot continue reading it or you get lost trying, most likely the author and you fall on opposite ends of the range for principle 5 (the thinking continuum). You and the author have a common interest—the subject of the book—but the way you understand other people's ideas does not match the writer's way of thinking and communicating those ideas to her readers.

The same phenomenon occurs with spoken communication. Imagine you are in a seminar on an interesting topic. While listening to the speaker, you cannot keep your eyes open, and you begin to fall asleep. You and the speaker are most likely at the opposite ends of the thinking continuum. The speaker's way of thinking is the opposite of your own, which turns even a good speech on an interesting topic into sleepy noise for you. Clearly, this is not an efficient way for you to learn!

This scenario has a corollary on the home front, which bears remembering: if you and your loved one are at opposite ends of the thinking continuum, do not be like that author or lecturer you can't follow! Don't try to explain your feelings or the good intentions behind some of your "wrong actions" to your loved one. Simply say you're sorry and move on. If you try to explain yourself, you will either notice a confused face or an unhappy face. You'd better stop as soon as you can. The more you try to explain the worse it will get. The other person won't be able to understand you but will get more annoyed or even become angry—much like how you probably felt while trying to follow the author or lecturer I just described. Neither way of thinking or communicating is wrong or even preferable; they're just entirely different, much like if you were explaining something in Mandarin to someone who only spoke Italian.

On the other hand, when we communicate with people who are in a similar place on the scale for principle 5/the thinking continuum, we sometimes find ourselves finishing each other's sentences. In these situations, even though you are interrupting each other's speech at times, the conversation feels fun and exciting to both participants. This is because you're not actually cutting off each other's *thoughts*. You have a very similar way of thinking. You both are at the same spot along the thinking continuum.

Being at the same place on principle 5 (the thinking continuum) doesn't mean you'll always agree. Sometimes people argue. If two people are at the same place on this continuum, they can feel completely satisfied and at peace even after arguing or raising their voices at each other. One person may have convinced the other, or both may have agreed on a compromise. Both people feel fine because of their common way of thinking and communicating those thoughts.

However, when a couple starts talking about something small but ends up in a big fight, causing one or both sides to feel frustrated, they are on the opposite sides of principle 5. These couples need to learn to accept each other, agree to disagree, and move on as quickly as possible. If the matter must be resolved, try a different way of communicating it later on.

It's worth reiterating two additional observations about the ways principles 4 (giving) and 5 (thinking) often present themselves. First, individuals who are near either end of the continuums for both principle 4 and principle 5 are likely to be leaders, as we just saw in the discussion of politicians. These people can be very powerful and potentially also destructive. Second, individuals who are near the middle of the scale for principle 4 and principle 5 are less likely to be leaders. They are more talented as coaches or educators due to their ability to understand and work with a diverse range of personalities.

I'll end this chapter with some interesting stories from my own life.

Years ago, when my daughter, Janet, was a teenager, she had some difficulties with some of the tennis coaches I had hired to work with her. From time to time, I had to step in as a mediator between her and her coaches. One of these relationships was simply too difficult to be workable no matter how hard I tried. However, there was one coach I found for Janet who became very close to her. They seemed to have a father-daughter type of relationship that worked for both of them, and I never worried about it or got involved. Now that I have my theory, it is very clear to me that I was the reason for Janet's difficulties with the "problem" coaches! Since Janet and I have opposite personalities for communication, the coaches I chose for her were all people with whom I would like to work, as most of them thought the way I thought. Since Janet and I (and the coaches I picked for her) are so different in this regard, it was very difficult for Janet and the coaches to communicate—of course!

Being a teenager, Janet still relied on my guidance and my opinions for important matters. In fact, I hired her first coach because I couldn't coach Janet myself; not only am I not a tennis pro (or a coach), but Janet and I have such different personalities. Because Janet and I have opposite personalities when it comes to thinking and communication, we often had arguments on the tennis court when I was trying to be her coach. Sometimes we had to stop practice soon after we started because of these conflicts. In hindsight, I realize I should have chosen the coaches I had trouble working with. David—the coach she became so close to—likely falls near the midpoint of the continuum for the thinking personality since he communicated easily with both Janet and me. We both love him very much. The other coaches were probably much closer to my way of thinking, which didn't work well for Janet and often required my intervention to get things sorted out. If my theory had been available to me back then, I would have chosen tennis coaches for her differently, and it would have been more productive for her.

My theory did help me predict the reactions of people in relationships effectively or with a somewhat high probability of success.

From time to time, when talking with my patients, I have made a prediction of the reactions of their loved ones about their relationship issues. They were always surprised that I was right and asked me how I knew these things. I told them my theory helped me as well as the answers they had provided to the questions you will find in chapter 11. I would then share my ideas that might help them resolve their relationship issues. These ideas made sense to my patients, who found them helpful.

Perhaps surprisingly, this same approach worked with my own daughter. When Janet was in high school, she sometimes asked me for ideas about relationship issues she was experiencing with her schoolmates or friends. I would suggest what she might say and predict what the responses or results might be. Most of the time, these predictions came true. When Janet asked me how I could have known what the results would be, I would reply, "I have my theory." This planted the seed, and before long, she asked to learn the theory herself. Later, during the most difficult time in our relationship, Janet still found the theory helpful and used it. We fought a lot, but we truly respected each other. We know we each have something the other one does not have. We love each other, but even with my theory, we still have to remind ourselves to keep a proper distance so we can avoid unnecessary fights. We chose to work closely together to achieve a higher potential, and we learned how to do it…although I would not suggest our personality combination for a long-term romantic relationship!

Chapter 11

Identifying Your Personalities

This chapter includes a comprehensive questionnaire to help you identify the various sides of your own personalities.

In chapter 4, we explored the personality for giving and receiving; this personality is addressed by questions 1 through 18 in this questionnaire. In chapter 5, we looked at ways of thinking; questions 19 through 36 will help you identify this aspect of your personality in this regard. Finally, we examined the various aspects and ways of loving in chapter 6; questions 37 through 60 will help you identify your love personality level of emotional, sexual, and nonsexual intimacies. The statements are divided into three tables (11.1 through 11.3), with one for each of these three principles.

In the tables, read each statement and put a circle in the box that best reflects how much you agree or disagree with each statement. (If a box has letters or numbers in it, circle around them; these will be explained in the answer key.) Reading from left to right, the response options include strongly disagree, disagree, neutral (neither agree nor disagree), agree, and strongly agree. There are no right or wrong answers.

Instructions for interpreting your results follow the quiz.

Please remember, this questionnaire and the analysis that follows are my own, which are based on my experiences and the theory described in this book. They are not intended to be prescriptions or cures for personal and relationship problems or to determine behavior; *they are only guideposts to help identify possible aids or directions to address conflicts and dilemmas.* For inextricable conflicts, professional therapists should be consulted.

THE THEORY OF TRUE LOVE

Table 11.1

1=Strongly Disagree, 2=Disagree, 3=Neutral, 4=Agree, 5=Strongly Agree

	Questions for the Giving and Receiving Personality	1	2	3	4	5
1	I help my partner as much as I can even if it is inconvenient for myself.					
2	I expect my partner to help me.					
3	I help my partner only when I want to.					
4	I do not want to be helped unless I ask for it.					
5	I like to help others as much as I can even if I may have to make self-sacrifices.					
6	I treat my partner's problems as my own.					
7	I expect my partner to treat my problems as their own.					
8	I am usually willing to adjust my schedule to accommodate my partner.					
9	I feel guilty if I do not help my partner when I am needed.					
10	I prefer exercising by myself instead of with my partner.					
11	I would rather do chores with my partner than by myself.					
12	I prefer to take care of things by myself instead of asking for help.					
13	It is easier for me to ask someone for directions than to figure them out myself.					
14	I prefer to compete as an individual rather than as a part of a team.					
15	I would rather spend time going to a party than spend time alone.					
16	I expect a favor back after I give one.					
17	I feel obligated to return a favor after I receive one.					
18	I prefer to work with people who are more enthusiastic than I am.					

Table 11.2

1=Strongly Disagree, 2=Disagree, 3=Neutral, 4=Agree, 5=Strongly Agree

	Questions for the Thinking Personality	1	2	3	4	5
19	After I have an argument with someone, I prefer to discuss and resolve the issue right away.					
20	When working on a project, I prefer to start by completing a small task instead of tackling the whole thing.					
21	I would rather learn to solve a problem by seeing examples than by learning the concept behind it.					
22	I prefer multiple-choice questions to essay questions or ones that require an explanation.					
23	When driving fast, I feel comfortable following the car in front of me very closely.					
24	I will not adjust my driving even if the car behind me follows my car very closely.					
25	I prefer to learn a physical activity by having someone show me instead of explaining it in words.					
26	I remember a concept better by understanding it rather than by visualizing it.					
27	I always walk as fast as possible to cross a street if a car stops for me.					
28	I usually do things at the last minute.					
29	I perform better in competitions than in practice.					
30	It is easier for me to remember a sequence of events than to remember names.					
31	I like to discuss relationship issues.					
32	When there is a conflict, I often try to put it away and forget about it.					
33	I like to ask questions during class.					
34	I usually prepare for exams and presentations as early as possible.					
35	I like to let the cars behind me pass even if I have to stop on the side.					
36	I don't like to debate.					

THE THEORY OF TRUE LOVE

Table 11.3

1=Strongly Disagree, 2=Disagree, 3=Neutral, 4=Agree, 5=Strongly Agree

	Questions for the Love Personality	1	2	3	4	5
37	I prefer holding my partner's hands rather than discussing our relationship issues.				1I	2I
38	It is more important for me to express my love through words than through cuddling.				1E	2E
39	If I have to choose between cuddling and sex, I would choose to cuddle.				1I	2I
40	I prefer having sex with my partner over hearing from my partner that they love me.				1S	2S
41	I feel happier when my partner initiates sex more often than holding hands.	-2S	-1S		1S	2S
42	I feel happier when my partner initiates holding hands more often than sex.	-2I	-1I		1I	2I
43	I love to hear my partner tell me how much they love me when we are intimate.	2I	1I		1E	2E
44	I prefer to have sex at least twice a week.	-2S	-1S		1S	2S
45	I prefer to have sex every day.				8S	9S
46	I often express my love during sex with words or kissing.	2S	1S		1E	2E
47	I want my partner to be selfless during sex.	2I	1I		1S	2S
48	Sometimes I have difficulty disagreeing with others in order to avoid hurting their feelings.	-2I	-1I		1E	2E
49	I feel happy to know my partner is always thinking of me.	-2E	-1E		1E	2E
50	I am easily brought close to tears when I watch emotional movies.	-2E	-1E		6E	8E
51	My partner's good intentions are more important to me than what actually happens.	-2E	-1E		1E	2E
52	I would consider staying with my partner if they had an affair for a short time, we discussed it, and the affair ended.				1I	2I

Table 11.3

1=Strongly Disagree, 2=Disagree, 3=Neutral, 4=Agree, 5=Strongly Agree

	Questions for the Love Personality	1	2	3	4	5
53	I would consider an open marriage if my spouse and I had very different sexual needs.				1I	2I
54	It is important for my partner to know my feelings of love toward them.	−2E	−1E		1E	2E
55	I am sensitive to my partner's feelings toward me.	−2I	−1I		1I	2I
56	I feel happy if my partner is in a good mood.	−2E	−1E		1E	2E
57	I like my good intentions to be understood by my partner even when I make a mistake.	−2E	−1E		1E	2E
58	I often try to assess what my partner is feeling.	−2I	−1I		1I	2I
59	When I go for a walk with my partner, I love to hold hands.	−2I	−1I		6I	8I
60	If I believe someone did something wrong, I would confront them, even in front of other people.	2I	1I		−1I	−2I

THE THEORY OF TRUE LOVE

To identify your personality levels for giving and receiving, tally your answers in each column of Table 11.1. *The first line that matches your results is your personality for giving and receiving.*

- If at least six of your answers are *strongly disagree*, you are at G1.
- If at least six of your answers are *strongly agree*, you are at G5.
- If at least six of your answers are *neutral*, you are at G3.
- If at least six of your answers are *disagree*, you are at G2.
- If at least six of your answers are *agree*, you are at G4.
- Otherwise, you are at G3.

To identify your personality levels for thinking, tally your answers in each column of Table 11.2. *The first line that matches your results is your personality for thinking.*

- If at least six of your answers are *strongly agree*, you are at T1.
- If at least six of your answers are *strongly disagree*, you are at T5.
- If at least six of your answers are *neutral*, you are at T3.
- If at least six of your answers are *agree*, you are at T2.
- If at least six of your answers are *disagree*, you are at T4.
- Otherwise, you are at T3.

To identify your personality levels for love (emotional, sexual, and nonsexual intimacy), the simplest way is to check the definition list in chapter 6 (see page 53-54). After answering all questions in table 11.3, you may have a good idea about where you fall on the three continuums of the love personality. To find out more specifically, separately tally all the numbers given for letters *E*, *I*, and *S* from all the boxes that you circled in table 11.3.

For your *E* score,

- if you scored more than 10, you have a high need for emotional intimacy; and
- if you scored less than 1, you have a low need for emotional intimacy.
- Otherwise, you have an average or moderate need for emotional intimacy.

For your *I* score,

- if you scored more than 10, you have high need for nonsexual intimacy; and
- if you scored less than 1, you have a low need for nonsexual intimacy.
- Otherwise, you have an average or moderate need for nonsexual intimacy.

For your *S* score,

- if you scored more than 10, you have a high need for sexual intimacy; and
- if you scored less than 1, you have a low need for sexual intimacy.
- Otherwise, you have an average or moderate need for sexual intimacy.

About the Author

Yaping Chen LAc was born and raised in China and moved to the United States in her late twenties. Her experiences in these two countries, with opposing political systems, served as an important foundation for her throughout her development of her theory of true Love. During her life, she experienced a "life and death" breakup, which allowed her to first begin developing her theory, which started with only four principles. Later on in her life, while she overcame the challenges of her second marriage and while raising her only daughter, she was able to complete her theory of true love with six principles.

Yaping believes that it is important to treat both physical and mental health at the same time to reach the best treatment outcome. Applying her theory of true love during her acupuncture treatments allows her treatments to be more effective by helping her patients simultaneously improve both their physical and mental well-being. She is passionate to continue her research and further the development of her theory for applications in children's education, romantic relationships, familial relationships, and management systems.

CPSIA information can be obtained
at www.ICGtesting.com
Printed in the USA
BVHW040239210522
637574BV00002B/11